THE LIBRARY OF CONGRESS
ITS ARCHITECTURE AND DECORATION

THE CLASSICAL AMERICA SERIES IN ART AND ARCHITECTURE
Henry Hope Reed and H. Stafford Bryant, Jr., *General Editors*

The American Vignola by William R. Ware
The Architecture of Humanism by Geoffrey Scott
The Classic Point of View by Kenyon Cox
The Decoration of Houses by Edith Wharton and Ogden Codman, Jr.
The Golden City by Henry Hope Reed
Fragments from Greek and Roman Architecture
    The Classical America Edition of Hector d'Espouy's Plates
Man as Hero: The Human Figure in Art by Pierce Rice (in preparation)
Monumental Classic Architecture in Great Britain and Ireland by Albert E. Richardson

THE CLASSICAL AMERICA PERIODICAL
    Classical America IV, edited by William A. Coles

With the Architectural Book Publishing Company

Student's Edition of the *Monograph of the Work of McKim, Mead & White, 1879–1915*
Student's Edition of *Paul Letarouilly's Buildings of Renaissance Rome* (in preparation)

Classical America is the society which encourages the
classical tradition in the arts of the United States.
Inquiries about the society should be sent to Classical
America, in care of W. W. Norton & Company, Inc.,
500 Fifth Avenue, New York, N.Y. 10110

THE LIBRARY OF CONGRESS

ITS ARCHITECTURE AND DECORATION

By HERBERT SMALL

EDITED BY HENRY HOPE REED

FOREWORD BY DANIEL J. BOORSTIN,
THE LIBRARIAN OF CONGRESS

PREFACE BY ARTHUR ROSS
INTRODUCTION BY PIERCE RICE

CLASSICAL AMERICA
THE ARTHUR ROSS FOUNDATION

W·W·NORTON & COMPANY
New York · London

Library of Congress Cataloging in Publication Data

Small, Herbert.
   The Library of Congress, its architecture and
decoration.

   1. Library of Congress.   I. Reed, Henry Hope.
II. Title.   III. Series.
Z733.U6S6   1982   027.573   82–14199

W. W. Norton & Company, Inc., 500 Fifth Avenue, New York, N.Y. 10110
W. W. Norton & Company Ltd., 37 Great Russell Street, London WC1B 3NU

ISBN 0 393 01587 4
ISBN 0 393 30038 2 (pbk.)

1 2 3 4 5 6 7 8 9 0

CONTENTS

LIST OF ILLUSTRATIONS

9

Also see floor plans in back of the book.

I.   The Library of Congress (Thomas Jefferson Building) viewed from the south-
     west across Independence Avenue and First Street.

II. *The Neptune Fountain. Neptune, with his trident, between two tritons blowing conch shells. The central group of the splendid fountain by Roland Hinton Perry, which is below the Library terrace on First Street.*

III. **The Art of Printing** *by Frederick MacMonnies. The central bronze door of the main entrance to the Library. The lunette depicts Minerva diffusing the products of the Typographical Art.*

IV.   The Vestibule of the Main Entrance in white marble, white stucco, and gilding.
      The figures of Minerva by Herbert Adams adorn voluted brackets. Note the
      pattern of the marble floor.

V. *Below, on the first floor, can be seen the Commemorative Arch with the spandrel figures by Olin Levi Warner. The corridor beneath leads to the Rotunda Reading Room. Above is the stairway going to the Visitors' Gallery, with the mosaic of Minerva by Elihu Vedder.*

VI. *The Main Entrance Hall showing the South Staircase with the varied sculpture by Philip Martiny.*

VII.   *Detail of the Main Entrance Hall ceiling. At each corner of the coved ceiling are two winged figures holding a cartouche with a lamp and book, symbols of learning. They are the work of Philip Martiny. Note the blue of the cove flecked with stars.*

VIII.   *The North Corridor off the Librarian's Room. A series of white marble bays with richly embellished domes. The murals of this corridor, not shown in the picture, are by Edward Simmons.*

X. *A section of the underside of an arch in the North Corridor near the Librarian's Room. Coffering with gold rosette and ground of gray, red, and blue with the detail in gold.*

IX. *The underside of an arch and a dome in the North Corridor near the Librarian's Room.*

XI.   Minerva *by Elihu Vedder at the landing of the stairs leading to the Visitors' Gallery of the Rotunda Reading Room.*

XII.   *The view west in the Rotunda Reading Room, showing the main entrance with, above, the great clock by John Flanagan and, above it in turn, the Visitors' Gallery.*

XIII.   *A Corinthian column and clustered piers with pilasters of the Rotunda Reading Room. They support a high broken entablature and a pendentive of the dome.*

XIV.   *The great dome of the Rotunda Reading Room, with its collar and lantern murals by Edwin Howland Blashfield. The ornament of the dome was executed by the sculptor Albert Weinert.*

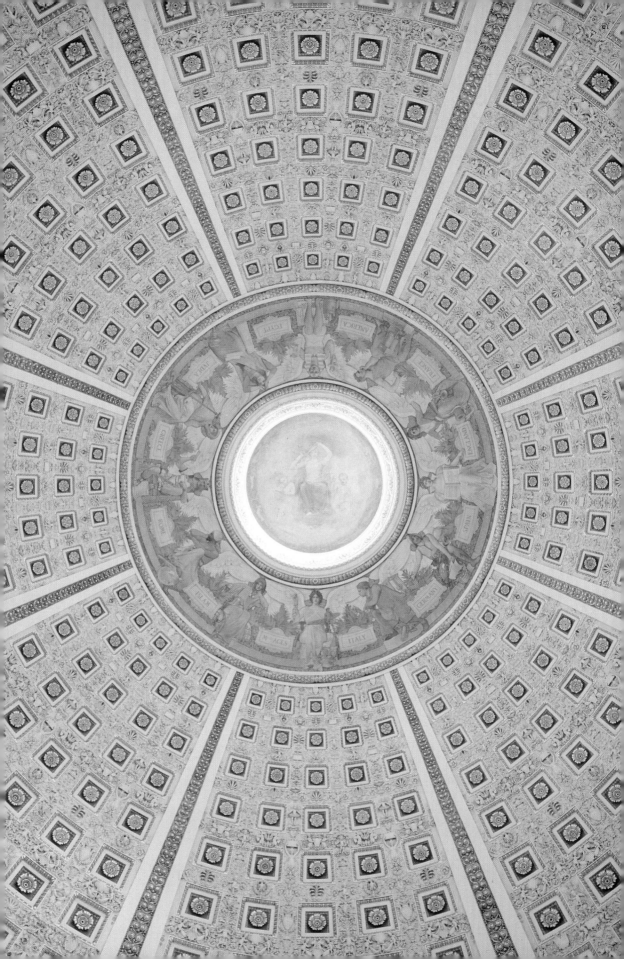

Photo: Anne Day

XV.   England, France, America, Egypt, *and* Judea, *five of the twelve figures in the collar of the dome by Edwin Howland Blashfield.*

XVI.   Romance, *with pen and scroll, in the East Corridor of the second floor by George Ran-
       dolph Barse, Jr. The printer's marks are those of the Brothers Sabio (right) and Melchior
       Sessa (left).*

XVII.   *Aglaia, one of the Three Graces, seen as the patroness of husbandry holding a shepherd's crook. Part of the vault mural in the South Corridor of the second floor by Frank Weston Benson.*

The original Library of Congress building—now named after Thomas Jefferson—is one of the grandest architectural monuments of nineteenth-century America. It is also, as this volume helps us discover, a vivid intellectual and artistic self-portrait of the United States at the turn of the century. There is no more comprehensive or more accessible catalogue of whom the builders of this monument believed to be the heroes of civilization. Here we read the names of the artists, scientists, authors, statesmen, and prophets whom they saw as their leaders up the paths of progress. We can read, too, the categories of civilization and the avenues of progress—law, science, literature, philosophy, and religion. We can share the moods and the myths that they most valued. We can see how they chose to embody these in portraits, panoramas, allegories, and decorative motifs.

We are grateful to Classical America and the Arthur Ross Foundation for this revision of Small's *Handbook*. And we remain grateful to Herbert Small himself for having provided the original text. No other national library in the world is more fortunate in its home. This volume helps us discover our good fortune and rediscover the grandeur that it is our duty and our opportunity to restore and to preserve.

Daniel J. Boorstin,
The Librarian of Congress

EDITOR'S ACKNOWLEDGMENTS

The editor is grateful for the welcome offered by Daniel J. Boorstin, the Librarian of Congress. He also appreciates the help extended by the Library's Information Office, the Publishing Office, the Library Environmental Resources Office, and the Library's Tour Office, and by Helen-Anne Hilker, formerly Interpretive Projects officer who is an authority on the history of the building, and Mary C. Lethbridge, formerly the Information officer who assisted Anne Day, the photographer, in many ways. He would also like to thank Robert Nikirk, librarian of the Grolier Club of New York for his assistance on printers' marks and names.

—HHR

The Library of Congress building, one of our nation's most imposing edifices, is appropriately located on the Capitol grounds opposite the wing of the House of Representatives. Completed in 1897, it was an exuberant affirmation of confidence by our government in our own heritage and in our future.

The library was originally founded in 1800, survived its burning by British troops in the War of 1812, was expanded by the absorption of the Thomas Jefferson Library, and, finally in 1886, an act of Congress provided for the construction of the present structure.

It reflects through sculpture and murals our cultural ancestry and the disciplines on which our civilization is based. Man's great achievements and intellectual conquests in such areas as medicine, law, physics, mathematics, theology, architecture, and zoology are portrayed through various forms of art often expressed allegorically and with an uplifting significance.

The decorative motifs in the reception areas and corridors of this vast building fittingly illustrate the principal means by which our civilization has evolved. Man's record is artistically communicated—the world of books encompassing our intellectual achievements is dramatically housed.

This new edition of Herbert Small's original *Handbook* of the Library of Congress in Washington, organized and sponsored by Classical America and the Arthur Ross Foundation, provides an appropriate occasion to reaffirm the ultimate truths inherent in a classical approach to the arts, welding together, as it does, the artistic talents of the sculptor, painter, and architect.

Herbert Small clearly captures this spirit. This revised edition, with new photographs and color plates, it is hoped, will be a beacon of light for our people and for visitors to our shores as we remind ourselves of our nation's cultural, artistic, and moral heritage.

September 1, 1981   *Arthur Ross*
New York City   15

Children can be coaxed or threatened into eating what they dislike, but the dislike remains. So it is with art. The viewer cannot be persuaded to enjoy sights that fail to move him. But when pleasure is felt, there may be some satisfaction in learning to whom we are indebted for this pleasure.

Accordingly, no effort will be made here to convince anyone of the beauty of the Library of Congress. It has one of the most splendid façades and, by all means, the richest interior in America. For that reason Classical America has singled out this guide to the Library of Congress to be represented in the Classical America Series in Art and Architecture.

The building is the finest flower of the era that embodies the principles the society stands for. The last decade of the nineteenth century saw the fulfillment in our country of the dream of the union of the arts. A now almost-forgotten world's fair, the World's Columbian Exposition at Chicago in 1893, had provided the example of painter, sculptor, and architect working side by side. The Library of Congress was the first great building that sprang out of the Chicago vision, to be followed by heroic civic projects with the state capitols, as a class, the most conspicuous and still the best known.

All these buildings remain popular and continue to be visited and enjoyed for themselves. But no single product of the age is viewed by such numbers as the Library. This is largely owed its location, in the very center of the city of Washington, across the street from the National Capitol itself. Still, if the visitor is brought into the Library out of duty or curiosity, surprise can only add to the pleasure offered by the spectacle of this fabulous structure. That pleasure is due to the perfect grasp by its builders of the necessity for all schemes of ornament to culminate in pictorial imagery and, by the same token, for that pictorial imagery to be displayed in settings especially prepared for it, an age-old rule of nature we have forgotten.

The Library's ornament—that is, the tiles, the mosaic, the rosettes, the columns and their capitals, the railings and balusters, pedestals and frames, the panels of leafage—is extremely beautiful, but this is secondary, in its effect on us, to its systematic arrangement. For the whole purpose of that ornament is to lead up to, and set out, figure sculpture and painting. And that sculpture and painting, however rewarding or disappointing in themselves, are infinitely richer by virtue of this progressive development.

In its essential character sculpture is architectural. Removed from its intended place, it is drained of half its force. Of sculpture conceived to begin with without a setting in view, society, in effect, is at a loss as to what to do with it. And the faint interest in sculpture, compared with pictures, of which the world is so fond, testifies to this.

But our keenness on pictures should not deceive us. It has little enough to do with art. In the higher context the same considerations are as true of painting as of sculpture. Where it belongs is in the particular spot for which it is prepared. The altarpiece is as ineffective on the museum wall as the faraway church from which it was taken is the poorer for its absence. We may love that picture, and others the church, but that each suffers from the separation is incontestable.

In short, the two great arts are of serious interest only in an architectural capacity, with all else dilettantism. That is, the responsibility of architecture, sculpture, and painting is nothing less than to make the works of man beautiful, and this is possible of realization only in combination with each other.

No better illustration of the rule in the matter exists than the building described in the book the reader now holds. It might be said that the very shortcomings of the carving and painting of the Library of Congress demonstrate the point made, for the measure of that work is not individual merit, but the brilliance and splendor that are owed its presence.

In no other American structure has it been more clearly understood by its designers that the pleasure a building provides us is fully satisfying only when it is capped by pictorial imagery. For three-dimensional ornament fulfills its role only when it leads up to the human figure in the round, and color remains no more than protective coating except when it is made use of to convey ideas. By the same token, it is equally urgent that the artist's most serious labors be enhanced by an ensemble of which they are a part. The American painter George de Forest Brush described the artist's true task to be the painting of "a noble subject on a wall."

The Library was the fine flower of an age with a bias toward ornament. What sets it apart from other generously carved and painted buildings in the United States is the systematic distribution of its carving and painting. The building is based on a plain, clear plan of which the spectacular Main Entrance Hall, opening toward the four corner pavilions and the Reading Room, is the center. But the simplicity of the plan only emphasizes the richness of the treatment of the balconies, corridors, halls, galleries, pavilions, and staircases. This richness is owed not the quality of the ornament, nor the material from which it has been wrought, nor the skill of its execution, though all these are of a very high order, but to the leading up from repeated forms to individualized ones. The moldings, the rosettes, the panels of leafage, the capitals, subtly distinguished from one another, culminate in the great bronze or marble single figures and groups, just as the gilding, the mosaic, and the stenciling prepare us for the sets of painted medallions and octagons. And these last are climaxed by the lunettes of the long galleries and the saucer domes of the pavilions, with the core of the whole being the crown of painting at the summit of the dome of the Reading Room. The painting and carving, besides making a dynamic unit of the Library's scheme, are all the more satisfactory by virtue of their fixed relation to setting, as principal ornaments in a graduated organization of ornament.

This book spells out the themes chosen by or assigned to the artists. If, at first glance, the central motif would appear to be literature, appropriate enough for a library, this is a stipulation very lightly adhered to, although the organization of the subject matter, the iconography, is very impressive. Signs of the zodiac are found in a floor or on a dome, Fire and War and Anarchy are among the subjects of the lunettes. But it should be noted that the true theme of the work is that central preoccupation of the plastic expression of Western civilization, the Celebration of Man, represented in pictorial terms by the human body. In that light the success of individual examples is to be measured by the grandeur of conception shown in the treatment of the figure. The methods to attain this artists and other specialists may deduce, guess at, and expatiate on, but the impact of the result registers alike on all of us.

Expertise has nothing to do with the matter. The sole standard is the degree by which we are moved. Critical comment is superfluous; our instincts determine our judgment. Accordingly, the chief usefulness of this guide is to give credit where it is due. The creation of the Library was a heroic achievement, and those principally responsible for it are, by all rights, great artists. If their names are unfamiliar, that reflects not on them but on the prevailing critical estimates which set store by lesser goals than fundamental ones.

The identities of those responsible for this triumph, completed in the closing years of the last century, were compiled by a little-known Boston newspaperman, Herbert Small. His book was published originally with the title *Handbook to the New Library of Congress in Washington,* and it appeared in 1897, the year the building was completed. What the reader will learn from Small are the names of the artists who painted the circular and octagonal medallions on the corridor ceilings, the large ceilings of the North, South, East, and West Pavilions, the lunettes that line the halls, and the painting in the Reading Room. Similarly, he has listed the modelers of the great Neptune Fountain that stands before the main façade of the Library, the bronze doors of the entrance, the busts of the nine writers chosen to preside over the Entrance Porch, and the immense quantity of sculpture within the Library.

But the Library is so transcendingly beautiful as an entity that it should be evident that the overriding artistic success arrived at was not that of even the most accomplished of the individual participants but of the marshaling of their combined efforts. The army of painters and sculptors who labored at the Library, most of whom of necessity remain anonymous, had to be led. The responsibility devolved on two men, Elmer Ellsworth Garnsey and Albert Weinert, who were the directors, respectively, of color and of sculpture. It fell to Garnsey's lot to supervise every inch of the setting of tiles, the gilding of the rosettes, the assembling of the mosaics, the lettering of mottoes and monograms, the laying on of acres of flat hues, and the invention and execution of the painted panels that are the chief features of the entire undertaking. At the same time Weinert bore the responsibility for everything touched by the chisel or shaped into any form of relief. Every molding, every baluster, the panels of ornament, the surface of the dome, the coffers of the dome and the ceilings, the exterior and interior capitals, the bronze doors, came within his jurisdiction as well as the great freestanding sculpture. If the Library, as we know it, could not have been brought into being without the wealth of talent that was lavished on it, the unparalleled result was due the directing of that talent toward a single end.

It is this last which distinguishes the Library from the great decorated buildings of the same era. Only a handful of state capitols and courthouses so much as approach comparison, and where they do is in the quantity of ornament, painting, and sculpture, not the fineness of their distribution. We go into these impressive buildings to see the works of art that make them what they are. The Library is itself the work of art we are here to savor.

A NOTE AS TO THIS NEW EDITION. The text of the Classical America edition, which is based on the 1901 edition of Herbert Small's *Handbook of the New Library of Congress in Washington,* has been edited and reset and the book given a new title. To make the guide more useful, there have been inserted descriptions of the additions to the building, now known as the Thomas Jefferson Building, and brief descriptions of the two annexes, the John Adams Building and the James Madison Memorial Building. New illustrations have been specially taken by Anne Day, supplemented by photographs from the collection of the Library. A biographical dictionary of those involved in the building's embellishment has been compiled and an illustrated glossary of art terms prepared. All of this was made possible by the generous help and guidance of the Arthur Ross Foundation.

THE LIBRARY OF CONGRESS
ITS ARCHITECTURE AND DECORATION

THE LIBRARY OF CONGRESS

The Library of Congress in Washington is not the mere reference library for the legislative branch of the government that its name would imply. It is, in effect, the library of the whole American people, directly serving the interests of the entire country. It was, it is true, founded for the use of the members of the Senate and House of Representatives; but, although the original rule still holds,★ the institution is a library as comprehensively national as the British Museum in London (now called the British Library), the Bibliothèque Nationale in Paris, or the National Library in Vienna. It is more freely open to the public than any of these, everyone of suitable age being permitted to use its collections without the necessity of a ticket or formal permission, while in scope it is their equal.

Its aim in the accumulation of books is inclusive and not exclusive. By the operation of the copyright law, any publisher, author, or artist desiring to obtain an exclusive privilege of issuing any publication whatever, must send two copies of the publication on which a copyright is asked to the Librarian of Congress to be considered for inclusion in the Library. Since 1870 the Library has been enabled to accumulate approximately the entire current product of the American press, as well as an enormous number of photographs, engravings, and other works coming under the head of fine arts. The possession of this material alone has given the Library a special national character.

★ Besides lending books to members of Congress, the Library lends research books through interlibrary loan to other libraries, including the research libraries of government agencies for use in advanced research. Some material, such as local history, genealogy, and irreplaceable materials, are not lent. The Library's Photoduplication Service provides photoduplicates of such materials, provided they are not subject to copyright or other restrictions.

See floor plans in the back of the book

The Library of Congress was founded in the year 1800, at the time the seat of government was moved to Washington. Five thousand dollars was the first appropriation, made April 24, 1800, while Congress was still sitting in Philadelphia. President John Adams signed the bill that included the provision for the Library. His successor, Thomas Jefferson, who assumed office on March 4, 1801, was especially in favor of it. He called it, later in life, with a sort of prophetic instinct, the "Library of the United States," and his support of it from the very beginning was so hearty and consistent that he may perhaps be regarded in the broad sense as the real founder of the institution.

The Library was shelved from the first in a portion of the Capitol building. The first catalogue was issued in April, 1802. It appears that there were then, in accordance with the old-fashioned method of dividing books according to size, not subject, 212 folios, 164 quartos, 581 octavos, 7 duodecimos, and 9 maps.

The Burning in the War of 1812

The War of 1812 wrecked the slender accumulations of the first dozen years of the Library's existence. The collection was entirely destroyed by fire by the British troops, which entered Washington August 24, 1814. The burning is described by a writer in an old magazine. "The British," he says, "first occupied the Capitol, only the two wings of which were finished, and connected by a wooden passageway erected where the Rotunda now stands. The leading officers entered the House of Representatives, where Admiral Cockburn of the Royal Navy (who was co-operating with General Ross), seating himself in the Speaker's chair, called the assemblage to order. 'Gentlemen,' shouted he, 'the question is, Shall this harbor of Yankee democracy be burned? All in favor of burning it will say Aye!' There was a general affirmative response. And when he added, 'Those opposed will say Nay,' silence reigned for a moment. 'Light up!' cried the bold Briton; and the order was soon repeated in all parts of the building, while soldiers and sailors vied with each other in collecting combustible material for their incendiary fires. The books on the shelves of the Library of Congress were used as kindling for the north wing; and the much admired full-length portraits of Louis XVI. and his queen, Marie Antoinette, which had been presented by the unfortunate monarch to Congress, were torn from their frames and trampled under foot. Patrick Magruder, then Clerk of the House of Representatives and Librarian of Congress, subsequently endeavored to excuse himself from not having even attempted to save the books; but it was shown that the books and papers in the departments were saved, and that the Library might have been removed to a place of safety before the arrival of the British."

Jefferson was then living in retirement at Monticello. He was in some financial difficulty at the time, and he offered the government the largest portion of his library, comprising some 6,700 volumes, for the price which he had originally paid for them—$23,950. The offer was accepted by Congress, although it met with much opposition. Among those who objected to the bill was Daniel Webster, then a representative from New Hampshire; while Cyrus King, a Federalist member of the House from Massachusetts, who "vainly endeavored to have provision made for the rejection of all books of an atheistical, irreligious, and immoral tendency"—a curious example of the many attacks of a similar nature made upon Jefferson by his political opponents.

The Acquisition of Jefferson's Library

With Jefferson's books as a nucleus, the Library of Congress began to make substantial gains. In 1832, a law library was established as a distinct department of the collection. In 1850, the Library contained about 55,000 volumes. On December 24, 1851, a fire broke out in the rooms in which it was shelved, consuming three-fifths of the whole collection, or about 35,000 volumes. A liberal appropriation for the purchase of books in place of those destroyed was made by Congress, and from that time to the present day the growth of the Library has been unchecked.

In December, 1864, Ainsworth Rand Spofford was appointed librarian by President Lincoln. The general management of the Library has always been in the hands of a joint committee of Congress; but the membership of the committee is constantly changing, so that the librarian is practically the real head and director of the institution. During the time that Spofford occupied his position, not

Development and Organization

only was the growth of the collection little short of marvelous, but so many changes of system were introduced as almost completely to transform the old Library of half a century ago. The year following Spofford's appointment, the previous copyright law was modified so as to require the deposit in the Library of Congress of a copy of every publication on which copyright was desired, the second copy required being deposited elsewhere. The administration of the law was still divided, however, in that each state had its own office for copyright—some states more than one—with the result that the volumes due the government were sometimes received and sometimes not. There was no way to call the negligent publisher or author to account, for no single office contained the complete information necessary. Such system as existed was often invalidated by the carelessness of the officials—the clerks of the United States District Courts—in charge of the various states. In 1870, therefore, Congress still further amended the copyright law by consolidating the entire department in the hands of the Librarian of Congress, as Register of Copyrights, and providing that of articles copyrighted, two copies are required to be deposited in the Library of Congress to perfect copyright.

The Old Quarters in the Capitol

For many years the Library had been kept in the west front of the Capitol. Here there was provision for perhaps 350,000 volumes. With the great increase, the old quarters had long been utterly inadequate. The crypts in the basement of the Capitol afforded room for storage, but the hundreds of thousands of books, pieces of music, and engravings thus stored were for the most part entirely inaccessible to the student—a serious loss to the usefulness of the Library, in spite of the fact that, so far as the books were concerned, only duplicates and such volumes as were seldom called for were thus laid away. The copyright business could be kept up-to-date only by the greatest effort. The rooms regularly devoted to the Library were so small, and so overcrowded with books, that there was almost no opportunity for quiet study, while the ordinary official routine was carried on with the greatest difficulty and inconvenience.

The New Building and After

With the decision to have a new building, the tremendous task of organizing the ever-expanding collection for the move to the new quarters devolved on Ainsworth Rand Spofford. The migration from the Capitol took place in 1897. That same year Spofford was succeeded as librarian by John Russell Young, the well-known journalist and diplomat. The Library of Congress began a life of its own.

The building has since undergone certain changes. Among them have been the installation of new rooms, such as the Coolidge Auditorium in 1927, the Rare Book Room in 1927, the Whittall Pavilion and the Hispanic Room in 1939, and the Poetry Room in 1951.

In addition two annexes have been built, one the John Adams Building opened in 1938 and the James Madison Memorial Building opened in 1980. With their coming, the main building has been named the Thomas Jefferson Building. For the general public this may appear confusing because, for visitors, the old building will always be the Library of Congress, which explains why the name has been retained for this guide.

THE LIBRARY OF CONGRESS— THE THOMAS JEFFERSON BUILDING

Ainsworth Rand Spofford, librarian from 1864 to 1897, had foreseen the inevitable accumulation and had proposed a special building for the Library as far back as 1871. Two years later, the Congress authorized a competition for a new library building, and, in December, 1873, the design of the firm of Smithmeyer and Pelz of Washington, D.C., was chosen out of a total of twenty-eight submissions. Then a long delay followed. Finally, on April 15, 1886, the Congress authorized the building's construction based on the winning design, and John L. Smithmeyer was named architect. In 1888 another act named Brigadier General Thomas Lincoln Casey, chief of engineers of the Army, in sole charge, subject to reporting directly to the Congress annually and to submitting plans to the secretary of war and the secretary of the interior. General Casey, to his death in 1896, had the entire responsibility for construction.

General Casey had been associated with the construction of some of the most important buildings undertaken by the government up to that time. They included the erection of the Executive Office (formerly State, War and Navy) Building and the completion of the Washington Monument. This last was an especially difficult task since it had been necessary to strengthen the old foundations of the shaft before proceeding with the work. Assisting him was Bernard Richardson Green, a civil engineer whom he now appointed superintendent and engineer of the Library building. John L. Smithmeyer was dismissed and his place taken by Paul J. Pelz. However, the original design was kept except for a few changes, and new drawings made.

The act of Congress of March 2, 1889, fixed the total cost at $6,245,567.94. Work continued and advanced to the point that the cornerstone was laid on August 28, 1890. Seven years later the building was ready to receive the Library's collections, and the total cost was $6,344,585.34.

The General Decoration Architects continued to change. Pelz, who had succeed Smithmeyer, was in turn dismissed in 1892 and replaced by Edward Pearce Casey, the general's son. In addition to his architectural duties, the younger Casey became adviser and superviser in matters of art. His designs were principally to include all of the most important interior architecture and the interior enrichment in relief and in color—in other words, the decoration that is the subject of this guide.

Two other men remain to be mentioned in giving any account of the building's construction: Elmer Ellsworth Garnsey, who was in charge, under the general supervision of the architect, of the color scheme of the interior, and Albert Weinert, who, in the same way, was in charge of the stucco ornamentation. The latter was put at the head of a staff of modelers who executed, on the spot, the great variety of relief arabesque and minor sculpture required in the comprehensive scheme adopted by Edward Pearce Casey, the stucco ornament being a chief factor in the decoration of the main halls and galleries throughout the building.

For the general decoration of the building—namely, all the painted ornament—Elmer E. Garnsey was responsible. He had done similar work at the World's Columbian Exposition of 1893 in Chicago, the Boston Public Library, and the Carnegie Library in Pittsburgh. A large studio was fitted up in the building, and a staff of designers and mural decorators organized. Edward J. Holslag was appointed foreman, William Andrew Mackay and Frederick C. Martin were employed to execute the finer portions of the designs, and W. Mills Thompson and Charles Caffin made the finished cartoons from the original sketches for the use of the mural painters. The latter numbered about twenty-five, and the larger portion of them were kept constantly busy for nearly a year and a half.

In addition, Edward P. Casey and Bernard R. Green, in 1894, consulted with the sculptors, John Quincy Adams Ward, Augustus Saint-Gaudens, and Olin Levi Warner on the sculpture needed for the Library's interior.

A year later the artists were chosen to execute the figurative mural decoration. In 1896 Edwin Howland Blashfield, the leading mural painter of the era, finished *The Evolution of Civilization* in the collar and the lantern of the dome. One more year passed, and all the mural work was completed, as was the mosaic of Minerva by Elihu Vedder near the entrance to the Visitors' Gallery of the Rotunda. On November 1, 1897, the building was thrown open to the public.

The great size of the building is perhaps best appreciated from a statement of the amount of some of the materials used in it: 409,000 cubic feet of granite, 500,000 enameled brick, 22,000,000 red brick, 3,800 tons of steel and iron, and 73,000 barrels of cement. The drafting office turned out, during the eight years that the Library was under construction, 1,600 plans and drawings. Exclusive of the cellar, the original floor space was 326,195 square feet, or nearly 8 acres; and the whole number of windows was about 2,165.

As a matter of "library economy," the arrangement of the building was of great interest at the time. The problems to be solved were mostly new ones. In a paper on the Library, read before the American Library Association, Bernard R. Green said: "Its design was preceded by few or no good examples of library architecture, and therefore the outcome of theory and deduction rather than the application of established principles." This task was not undertaken in any dogmatic way, however; "the effort was," as Green went on to say, "to plan on general rather than particular principles, and afford the largest latitude for expansion and re-arrangement in the use of the spaces."

The General Character of the Building

31

So far, however, as general interest is concerned, it is the magnificent series of mural and sculptural decorations with which the architecture its enriched that has contributed most to give the Library is notable position among American public buildings. Although a similarly comprehensive scheme of decoration was carried out at the World's Columbian Exposition of 1893 in Chicago, and afterward in the new Public Library in Boston, the government itself had never before called upon a representative number of American painters and sculptors to help decorate, broadly and thoroughly, one of its great public monuments. Commissions were here given to nearly *fifty sculptors and painters*—all Americans—and their work, as shown throughout the building, forms the most interesting record possible of the scope and capabilities of American art.

It may be noted here, also, that, both inside and out, the Library is, in the main, in the style of the Italian Renaissance—derived, that is to say, from the architecture of the buildings erected in Italy during the period (roughly speaking, the fifteenth century or earlier) when the elements of classical art were revived and recombined in a renascence, or new birth, of the long-neglected models of Greece and Rome.

THE EXTERIOR OF THE BUILDING

The site of the Library originally comprised two city blocks, containing seventy houses, with an extent, of 10 acres. It is bounded by First, East Capitol, and Second Streets, and Independence Avenue. The general effect of the grounds enclosing the Library is that of an extension of the Capitol grounds, the street separating the two, for example, being treated, so far as possible, as a driveway through a park.

The Library faces exactly west. It is 470 feet long (from north to south), and 340 deep (from west to east). It occupies, exclusive of approaches, 3¾ acres. (See Plate I, between pages 16 and 17.)

See floor plans in the back of the book

The general disposition of the building may best be seen by a glance at the ground plan. The exterior walls are thus seen to belong to a great rectangle, which encloses a cross dividing the open space within into four courts, each 150

32

feet long by 75 or 100 feet wide. At the intersection of the arms of the cross is an octagon, serving as the main reading room, and conspicuous by reason of its dome and lantern, which rising well above the walls of the Library, are the first feature of the building to attract the attention of the visitor. The lantern is surmounted by a great blazing torch with a flame, originally gilded—the emblematic Torch of Learning—which marks the center and apex of the building, 195 feet above the ground. The dome and the domed roof of the lantern were sheathed with copper, over which, with the exception of the ribs of the dome, left dark to indicate their structural importance, was laid a coating of gold leaf, 23 carats fine. The surface covered was so large that one's first thought was apt to be of the expense. As a matter of fact, however, the total cost—including the gilding for the flame of the torch—was less than $3,800.★ (The growth of the Library in the years following completion of the building made it necessary for two of the courts to be filled completely with bookstacks. A third was partially occupied by the Coolidge Auditorium and the Whittall Pavilion, but room was left for an attractive garden adjoining the Pavilion. The fourth court, in the southwest quarter of the building, survived occupation by temporary constructions at various times for offices and a cafeteria and is now a pleasant space for visitors and staff to read or rest.)

The exterior walls of the Library are constructed wholly of granite, quarried in Concord, New Hampshire. The stone is a close-grained variety, so even and light in tone that when the sun is shining upon it the effect is almost as brilliant as if a white marble had been used. The massive buttresses which support the Rotunda, as it is called although its shape is actually that of an octagon, at each of its eight corners, and so much of the Rotunda wall as is visible from the outside, are also granite, but of a different quality, slightly darker in hue, and coming from quarries in Maryland.

 The Library is in three stories: the basement story of 14 feet; the first story, or main library floor, of 21 feet; and the second story of 29 feet—making a height of 64 feet for

The Façades

★The gold leaf has long vanished. The lantern and the dome are a copper green.

Bronze lamp standard on the terrace, a triumph of classical detail from cherub's heads to acanthus leaves.

the three stories at the lowest point. Adding to this the base at ground level, and the simply designed balustrade which surmounts the whole, the total height is 72 feet above the ground. Beneath the entire structure is a cellar, below the level of the ground outside, but within opening upon the interior courts. The granite of which the walls are constructed is rough, or "rock-faced," in the basement story; much more finely dressed in the story above; and in the second story brought down to a perfectly smooth surface. The windows in the basement are square-headed, as also on the library floor, except along the west front, where they are arched, with ornamental keystones. Throughout the second story they are again square-headed, but with casings in relief, surmounted by pediments alternately rounded and triangular, and, along the west front, railed in at the bottom by false balustrades.

To prevent the monotony incident to a long, unrelieved façade, the walls are projected at each of the four corners and in the center of the east and west sides, into pavilions, which, in addition to being slightly higher than the rest of the rectangle—thus allowing space for a low attic story—are treated with greater richness and elaboration of ornamental detail. The corners are set with vermiculated granite blocks—blocks whose surface is worked into "vermiculations" or "worm tracks." The keystones of the window arches in the first story are sculptured with a series of heads illustrating the chief ethnological types of mankind. Along the second-story front runs a portico supported upon a row of twin columns, each a single piece of granite, with finely carved Corinthian capitals. The pedestals which support the columns are connected by granite balustrades, so that the portico forms a single long balcony, with an entrance through the windows which look out upon it.

THE ENTRANCE PAVILION

Of all these pavilions the Main Entrance Pavilion is by far the largest as well as the most ornate. It is 140 feet long, or almost a third the total length of the building, and about 7 feet higher than either of the other five pavilions. At either end it is itself projected, or pavilioned. The Main Entrance is through a porch of three arches, on the main library floor. The approaches are extensive and imposing. A flight of steps, constructed of granite from Troy, New Hampshire, ascends from either side to a central landing, laid with flags of red Missouri granite. Thence the stairway leads in a single flight to the Entrance Porch, with space underneath for a *porte cochère* or canopy in front of the doors admitting to the basement. The central landing just spoken of is protected by a high retaining wall which forms the background for a splendid fountain by Roland Hinton Perry, ornamented with a profusion of allegorical figures in bronze—the chief figure representing Neptune enthroned in front of a grotto of the sea.

The posts of the granite railing of the steps support elaborate bronze candelabra, bearing clusters of electric lamps for illumination at night. The spandrels of the Entrance Porch—the approximately triangular spaces flanking the three arches—are ornamented with female figures sculptured in high relief in granite, representing Literature, Science, and Art. They were modeled by Bela Lyon Pratt. Above the main windows of the Library floor is a series of smaller, circular windows, which serve as a background for a series of granite busts (the pedestals of which rest in the pediments below) of men eminent in literature. There are nine in all, seven along the front, and one at each end of the pavilion. They are flanked by boldly sculptured fig-

Photo: Anne Day

Winged cherub's head on the lamp standard of the terrace.

35

ures of children, reclining upon the sloping pediments or, alternately, by massive garlands of fruits. The keystones of the circular windows each support the standing figure of a winged cherub, all sculptured from a single design and introduced as the accentuating feature of a frieze of foliated ornament extending along the three sides of the pavilion. Like the garlands and figures on the pediments, they were modeled by William Boyd. At either end of the attic story Boyd's hand appears again in the sculptural embellishment of the little porch—as one may perhaps call it—which looks out upon the balcony formed by the granite railing. The rounded pediment contains a group in granite consisting of the American eagle flanked by two seated children. Each pediment is supported on the shoulders of two conventional Atlases—"Atlantides" is the technical name—figures of gigantic strength, so called because in the Greek and Roman mythology Atlas was fabled as a giant supporting the vault of heaven by his unaided strength.

A more particular description is required of the fountain, the ethnological heads, the series of busts in the portico of the Entrance Pavilion, and the spandrel figures ornamenting the Entrance Porch.

Roland Hinton Perry's Fountain

Of Perry's fountain (see Plate II, between pages 16 and 17), it may be said at once that it is one of the most lavishly ornamental in the country. It occupies a semicircular basin 50 feet broad, containing a dozen bronze figures disposed to represent a scene—so one may take it—in the court of Neptune, the classic god of the sea. The granite wall of the terrace against which the fountain is placed contains three deep niches, in the spandrels of which are six dolphins sculptured in relief from models by Albert Weinert. The niches themselves are treated with an evident suggestion of a grotto worn by the sea, with a hint, also, at the formation of stalactites by the constant dripping of water. In front of the central niche Neptune is seated in a majestic attitude on a bank of rocks. He is represented as an old man with a long, flowing beard, but the lines of his naked figure indicate the energy and great muscular strength befitting the Ruler of the Deep. The figure is of colossal size; it would be, that is, if standing, about 12 feet in height. On either side of the bank lolls a figure of Triton, one of the minor sea-gods, blowing a conch shell to summon the water deities to the throne of their sovereign. In front of each of the niches at the side is a sea nymph triumphantly bestriding an infuriated sea horse, his ears laid back and his fish's tail writhing with anger on account of a jet of water constantly thrown against his head. The basin is crossed and recrossed by similar jets, which furnish the whole flow of water, and proceed from the mouths of sea monsters in various places throughout the fountain. There are seven of them in all. The first is a serpent just showing itself above the water in front of the bank on which Neptune is seated. Higher up, to the right and left, two gigantic frogs lurk in crevices of the rocks; and floating along the outer edge of the basin are four huge Florida turtles, their heads raised a little above the water and their long fins making as if swimming.

The ethnological heads ornamenting the keystones of the first-story pavilion windows offer as interesting material for study as any of the decorations of the Library. The series is unique in that it is the first instance of a comprehensive attempt to make ethnological science contribute to the architectural decoration of an important public building. It was at first proposed to employ a more conventional kind of ornament, such as the familiar Gorgons' heads so often found in connection with Renaissance architecture. The present idea was carried out with the assistance of Otis T. Mason, the curator of the Department of Ethnology in the National Museum of Natural History. The heads, thirty-three in number, are about a foot and a half in height, and were modeled, some by William Boyd and others by Henry Jackson Ellicott, after data accumulated by Professor Mason as the result of some six months' special study of the ethnological collections in the possession of the museum—which contains, indeed, practically all the material (books, photographs, carefully verified measurements) necessary for such an undertaking.

Taking into consideration the difficulty of obtaining the more delicate differentiation of the features in a medium so unsatisfactory, from its coarseness of texture, as granite, the result of Professor Mason's work is one of the most scientifically accurate series of racial models ever made. Still another difficulty, it may be added, lay in the fact that each head had to be made to fit the keystone. Besides the neces-

The Ethnological Heads

sity of uniform size, the architect demanded also, as far as possible, a generally uniform shape, which it was often very hard to give and still preserve the correct proportions of the racial type. The face had to be more or less in line with the block it ornamented, and, especially, the top of the head had to follow, at least roughly, a certain specified curve. This last point was met either by using or not using a headdress, whichever best met the difficulty. In one case the problem was a little puzzling—that of the Plains Indian, with his upright circlet of eagle's feathers, which were bound to exceed the line, if accurately copied. The difficulty was frankly met by laying the feathers down nearly flat upon the head.

In preparing the models, accuracy was the chief thing considered. Any attempt at dramatic or picturesque effect, except what was natural to the type portrayed, was felt to be out of place. Each head was subjected to the strict test of measurement—such as the ratio of breadth to length and height, and the distance between the eyes and between the cheekbones—this being the most valuable criterion of racial differences. All portraiture was avoided, both as being somewhat invidious and unscientifically personal, and, more especially, because no one man can ever exemplify all the average physical characteristics of his race. On the other hand, the heads were never permitted to become merely ideal. It will be noticed that all are those of men in the prime of life.

The list of the races, beginning at the north end of the Entrance Pavilion, and thence continuing south and round the building to the Northwest Pavilion, is as follows, each head being numbered for convenience in following the order in which they occur: 1, Russian Slav; 2, Blond European; 3, Brunette European; 4, Modern Greek; 5, Persian

Photos: Anne Day

Ethnological heads found on the keystones of the main façade. From the top: Blond European, Arab, Turk, Modern Egyptian, Abyssinian, Zulu.

(Iranian); 6, Circassian; 7, Hindu; 8, Hungarian (Magyar); 9, Semite, or Jew; 10, Arab (Bedouin); 11, Turk; 12, Modern Egyptian (Hamite); 13, Abyssinian; 14, Malay; 15, Polynesian; 16, Australian; 17, Negrito (from Indian Archipelago); 18, Zulu (Bantu); 19, Papuan (New Guinea); 20, Sudan Negro; 21, Akka (Dwarf African Negro); 22, Fuegian; 23, Botocudo (from South America); 24, Pueblo Indian (as the Zuñis of New Mexico); 25, Esquimaux; 26, Plains Indian (Sioux, Cheyenne, Comanche); 27, Samoyede (Finnish inhabitant of northern Russia); 28, Korean; 29, Japanese; 30, Ainu (from northern Japan); 31, Burmese; 32, Tibetan; 33, Chinese.

It will be seen that the various races are grouped as far as possible according to kinship. There is not, however, space—and this is hardly the place—in which to explain the many points which might be brought up in connection with this interesting series of heads. For such information the reader is referred to any good textbook on ethnology. One or two special details, however, may properly be mentioned. The selection of the Pueblo Indian, for example, was a second choice. Professor Mason would have preferred one of the ancient Peruvian Incas, but no satisfactory portrait could be found to work on. The Tibetan is a Buddhist priest, as indicated by his elaborate turban. The Chinese belongs to the learned, or Mandarin, class. The Russian with his fur cap is the typical Slavic peasant. The Blond European is of the educated German type, dolichocephalic, or long-headed; the Brunette European is the Roman type, brachycephalic, or broad-headed. The architect has introduced a Greek fret on the turban of the Greek to symbolize the importance of ancient Greek art. The Egyptian is the typical Cairo camel-driver. The Korean wears the dress and hat of the courtier, and the Turk also

Ethnological heads found on the keystones of the main façade. From the top: Papuan, Pueblo Indian, Plains Indian, Japanese; bottom row, from left: Tibetan, Chinese.

39

is depicted as a member of the upper classes. The Hungarian wears the astrakan or lamb's wool cap of the peasant. Many of the heads are shown with peculiar ornaments—the Malay with his earrings, the Papuan with his nose plug, the Botocudo with studs of wood in his ears and lower lip, and the Esquimaux with the labret or lip plug of walrus ivory. The face of the Polynesian, finally, is delicately incised with lines, copied from a specimen of Maori (New Zealand) tattooing.

The Portico Busts The list of the men commemorated by the nine busts in the portico is as follows: Demosthenes, Emerson, Irving, Goethe, Franklin, Macaulay, Hawthorne, Scott, and Dante. The Demosthenes, Scott, and Dante were modeled by Herbert Adams; the Emerson, Irving, and Hawthorne by Jonathan Scott Hartley; and the Goethe, Franklin, and Macaulay by Frederick Wellington Ruckstull. The reader will see that as far as possible with an odd number, the work of each sculptor is, so to say, in balance—Rickstull's in the center, flanked by Hartley's, and Adams's at either end—thus avoiding any possible confusion of style, and giving the artist all the advantage which comes from a symmetrical disposition of his productions. There is, as a matter of fact, very little diversity in the present series. Each bust is of uniform height—about 3 feet, not reckoning the pedestal—with a uniform background. The statue of Franklin, coming in the center, has, intentionally, a certain effect of pre-eminence. The sculptor conceived him "as one of the greatest men of this country, and as a writer and philosopher the patriarch, and therefore aimed to make him dominate the rest." A word should be said regarding the background of the busts—the glass enclosed in the framing of the circular windows. The effect, as always of a window, is dark, as granite would not have been, thus throwing the busts, which are of the same material as the walls, into sharp, strong relief.

Bela Lyon Pratt's Spandrel Figures The beautiful spandrel figures of the Entrance Porch modeled by Bela Lyon Pratt are six in number. All are about life-size, and are shown leaning gracefully against the curve of the arches. After what has been said of the intractability of granite as a medium for any but the bolder sorts of sculpture, it is not out of place to call attention to the

Photo: Anne Day

Literature represented by two female figures, both holding books. Spandrels in the left arch of the Entrance Porch by Bela Lyon Pratt.

exceptional delicacy and refinement with which these figures have been chiseled. They represent, as has been said, Literature (the left-hand arch), Science (in the center), and Art (to the right). In the background of each spandrel the sculptor has introduced a branch of walnut, oak, laurel, or maple leaves. Of the figures themselves, the two to the left stand respectively for the contemplative and the productive sides of Literature—reflection and composition. The one is writing upon a tablet, although for a moment she turns aside as if in search of the fitting phrase; while the other, at the right, with a hood over her head and a book held idly in her hand, gazes out dreamily into the distance. Of the figures of Science, the first holds the torch of knowledge, and the second, with the celestial globe encircled by the signs of the zodiac in her arm, looks upward, as if to observe the courses of the stars. Here, also, something of the same distinction as in the first arch is drawn between the abstract and the practical. In the third group, the figure to the left represents Sculpture, and that to the right, Painting. The latter busies herself with the palette and brush. Sculpture, with a mallet in hand, is studying a block of marble in which she has already blocked out the head and features of a bust—that of Dante.

41

Tradition, a seated woman with a boy. On the left are a seated Norseman with axe and a shepherd with crook, and on the right an American Indian with arrows and a prehistoric man. Lunette of the left bronze door of the Main Entrance by Olin Levi Warner.

THE MAIN ENTRANCE

The three deep arches of the Entrance Porch terminate with three massive bronze doors, covered with a design of rich sculptural ornament in relief. Each is 14 feet high to the top of the arch, with an extreme width, including the framing, of 7½ feet, and a total weight of about 3½ tons. The subject of the decoration is, in the central door, The Art of Printing, modeled by Frederick MacMonnies; in the door to the left, Tradition, by Olin Levi Warner; and to the right, Writing, begun by Warner, but left unfinished at his death (in August, 1896), and completed by Herbert Adams. The three thus indicate in a regular series—the sequence of which, of course, is Tradition, Writing, and Printing—the successive and gradually more perfect ways in which mankind has preserved its religion, history, literature, and science. Each of the doors is double, with a lunette at the top closing the arch. The various portions of the design are comprised in a high and rather narrow panel in each leaf, with small panels above and below, and finally the large semicircular panel occupying the lunette above.

Olin Levi Warner's Bronze Doors

Warner's first door, Tradition, illustrates the method by which all knowledge was originally handed down from generation to generation. The background of the panel in the larger lunette is a mountainous and cloudy landscape, conveying admirably, says one critic, "a sense of prehistoric vastness and solitude." In the center is a woman, the

42

embodiment of the subject, seated on a throne. Against her knee leans a little boy, whom she is instructing in the deeds and worship of his fathers. The visitor will not fail to notice the unusual expressiveness of the group—the boy with eager, attentive face, and the woman holding his hand in one of hers, and raising the other in a gesture of quiet but noble emphasis. Seated on the ground, two on either side, and listening intently to her words, are an American Indian, holding a couple of arrows in his hand; a Norseman, with his winged steel cap; a prehistoric man, with a stone axe lying by his side; and a shepherd with his crook, standing for the nomadic, pastoral races. The four are typical representatives of the primitive peoples whose entire lore was kept alive by oral tradition. The face of the Indian is understood to be a portrait of Chief Joseph, of the Nez Percé tribe, from a sketch made from life by Warner in 1889.

Of the panels below, that to the left contains the figure of a woman holding a lyre, and the other the figure of a warrior's widow clasping the helmet and sword of her dead husband to her breast. The first represents Imagination, and the second Memory, the former being the chief quality which distinguishes the nobler sorts of traditional literature, as exemplified in the true epics, springing from the folk tales of the people, and the latter standing for that heroic past with which it so constantly deals.

The same general arrangement of figures is followed in the second door—the one representing Writing—as in the first. In the lunette of the door, a female figure is seated in the center, holding a pen in her hand and with a scroll spread open in her lap. Beside her stand two little children, whom she is teaching to read or write. To the right and left are four figures representing the peoples who have had the most influence on the world through their written memorials and literature—the Egyptian and the Jew to the right, and the Christian and Greek to the left. The Jew and the Christian are represented as kneeling, in allusion to the religious influence which they have exerted. The former holds a staff in his hand, and may be taken as one of the ancient Jewish patriarchs; the latter bears a cross. The Greek has a lyre, for Poetry, and the Egyptian holds a stylus in his hand.

The standing figures in the door proper are of women,

and represent Truth (on the left) and Research (on the right). Research holds the torch of knowledge or learning, and Truth a mirror and a serpent, the two signifying that in all literature, wisdom (of which the serpent is the emblem) and careful observation (typified by the mirror, with its accurate reflection of external objects) must be joined in order to produce a consistent and truthful impression upon the reader. The smaller panels below contain a design of conventional ornament with cherubs or geniuses supporting a cartouche, on which the mirror or serpent of the larger panels is repeated.

Frederick MacMonnies's Bronze Door

In MacMonnies's design the lunette is occupied by a composition which he has entitled Minerva Diffusing the Products of Typographical Art (see Plate III between pages 16 and 17). The goddess of learning and wisdom—a fit guardian to preside at the main portral of a great library—is seated in the center upon a low bench. On either side is a winged cherub, the messengers of the goddess, each carrying a load of ponderous folios which she is dispatching as her gift to mankind. To the right is her owl, perched solemnly on the bench on which she is sitting. She wears the conventional helmet and breastplate—the latter the aegis, with its Medusa's head—of ancient art, but in her wide, full skirt, with its leaf-figure pattern, the artist has adopted a more modern motive. The Latin title of MacMonnies's subject, *Ars Typographica,* and various symbolical ornaments are introduced in the background. To the right and left, enclosed in a laurel wreath, are a Pegasus and a stork. The former stands, for course, of the poetic inspiration which gives value to literature. The stork, commonly symbolizing filial piety, may be taken here, if one chooses, as typifying the faithful care of the inventors of printing and their disciples in multiplying the product of that inspiration. To the left, also, are an hourglass, an ink ball, and a printer's stick; and on the other side of the panel, an ancient printing press.

Each of the small panels in the upper portion of the doors below is in the shape of a rectangle, and is occupied by a conventionally decorative design composed of a wreath with floating ribbons, enclosing an ancient lamp, symbol of learning. Each of the upright panels contains the figure of a young and beautiful woman, clad in a robe of the same design as that worn by Minerva, and carrying two tall flaming torches. The figure in the left-hand leaf represents the Humanities, the soft contours of her face expressing the gentle and generous liberalities of learning. Her companion stands for Intellect, and the lines of her face are of a bolder and severer character.

THE MAIN ENTRANCE HALL

Entering by any one of these three bronze doors, one passes immediately through a deep arch into the Main Entrance Hall. It is constructed of gleaming white Italian marble, and occupies very nearly the whole of the Entrance Pavilion. By reason of a partial division of the hall into stories and open corridors, and on account of the splendor and variety of the decoration everywhere so liberally applied, the eye is attracted to a number of points of interest at once. The arrangement, however, is really simple and well defined, as is always true of great classical buildings. (See the plan at back of book.) With the exception of a portion of the attic story and of two or three small rooms partitioned off in the southeast and northeast corners of the first floor, the entire pavilion serves as a single lofty and imposing hall. In the center is a great well, the height of the pavilion—75 feet—enclosed in an arcade of two stories, the arches of the first supported on heavy piers and of the second on paired columns. The center of the well is left clear; on either side, north and south, is a massive marble staircase, richly ornamented with sculpture. On the east side of the pavilion a broad passageway, treated as a part of the general architectural scheme of the Main Entrance Hall—really an arm of the interior cross already referred to—connects it with the Main Reading Room Rotunda.

The Vestibule

The arcades surrounding the well, or Main Entrance Hall, as it would better be called, screen two stories of corridors. The corridor which the visitor has now entered—the West Corridor, on the library floor—serves as the general vestibule of the building, and appropriately, therefore, is more sumptuously decorated than any of the others. The most striking feature is a heavily paneled ceiling, finished in white

Decoration in the Main Vestibule.
The Minerva of War holding a short
sword in her left hand and, in her
right, the torch of learning. Herbert
Adams, sculptor.

Photo: Anne Day

*The Stucco Decoration
of the Vestibule*

and gold—perhaps as fine an example of gold ornamentation on a large scale as can be found in the country. It is impressively rich and elegant without in the least overstepping the line of modesty and good taste.

The corridor is bounded by piers of Italian marble ornamented with pilasters. There are four piers on each side, those on the west terminating the deep arches of the doors and windows, and one at either end. It will be noticed that these piers, like all the others on this floor, are wider than they are deep, so that the arches they support are of varying depth—the narrow ones running from north to south, and the deeper ones from east to west, invariably. This difference of depth, both of the piers and of the arches, is apt to be somewhat bewildering until one perceives the system on which it is based, so that it may be well to add in this connection that the same rule of broad and narrow, and the direction in which each kind runs, holds good, also, of the corridors on the second floor, the only variation being that paired columns, as has already been pointed out, are substituted for piers.

Above the marble arches of the Vestibule the wall with its ornamentation, and the whole of the paneled ceiling, are of stucco. By the use of this material, especially in connection with the gold, the architect has succeeded in obtaining a warmer and softer tone of white than would have been possible in marble.

Above each of the side piers are two white-and-gold consoles, or brackets, which support the paneled and gilded beams of the ceiling. In front of every console—and almost, but not quite, detached from it—springs a figure of Minerva, left in the natural white of the stucco. The figures are about 3 feet in height, and were executed from two different models, each the work of Herbert Adams (see Plate IV between pages 16 and 17). They are skillfully

46

composed in pairs: the first (the Minerva of War) carrying in one hand a falchion or short, stout sword, and in the other holding aloft the torch of learning; and the second (the Minerva of Peace) bearing a globe and scroll—the former significant of the universal scope of knowledge. Although thus differing, the figures are of the same type; both wear the aegis and the same kind of casque, and both are clad in the same floating classic drapery.

Modeled in relief upon the wall between the two Minervas is a splendid white-and-gold Roman tripod, used as an electric light standard. The bowl is lined with a circle of large leaves, from which springs a group of eight lamps, suggesting, when lighted, a cluster of some brilliant kind of fruit. Above the piers at either end of the corridor is another tripod, somewhat narrower and of a different design, but used for the same purpose.

It should be noted that, for the most part, both in the ceiling and on the walls, the gold has been dulled or softened in tone in order to avoid any unpleasing glare or contrast with the white. This effect, however, is regularly relieved by burnishing the accentuating points in certain of the moldings.

Before leaving the Vestibule, the visitor may be interested to notice the design of the marble flooring. The body of it is white Italian, with bands and geometric patterns of brown Tennessee, and edgings of yellow mosaic. It will be seen at once that the design is harmonious with the lines of the arcade and the ceiling. These are not slavishly mimicked, but are developed, varied and extended. Sometimes a circle is used to draw together two opposite arches; sometimes a square echoes the pattern of the ceiling; lines of beaming—as they may be called in an easy metaphor—connect opposite piers; and finally the boundaries of the corridor are outlined in a broad border enclosing the whole. It has been said that in hardly any other building in the country has so much pains been taken by the architect to make the lines of his floor designs consistent with those of the architecture and the general decorative scheme. Throughout the Library, wherever marble or mosaic is used for this purpose, the visitor will find this phase of the ornamentation of the building of the highest interest and importance.

The Marble Flooring

The Main Entrance Hall

Photo: Anne Day

Pisces, one of the signs of the Zodiac to be found in the marble floor of the Main Entrance Hall.

The floor of the Main Entrance Hall, into which one passes next, is an excellent example of this point. Besides the marble, the pattern contains a number of modeled and incised brass inlays. The one in the center is a large rayed disc, or conventional sun, on which are noted the four cardinal points of the compass, which coincide with the direction of the main axes of the Library. The disc thus performs the same service for the building—only more picturesquely and vividly—as an arrowhead cross for a chart or plan. From the sun as a center proceeds a great circular glory—or "scale pattern," as it is technically, and more descriptively, called—of alternate red and yellow Italian marble, the former from Verona and the latter from Siena. Other inlays are arranged in a hollow square, enclosing the sun as a centerpiece. Twelve represent the signs of the zodiac; the others are in the form of rosettes, in two patterns. They are embedded in blocks of dark red, richly mottled French marble, around which are borders of pure white Italian marble.

The Commemorative Arch

Photo: Anne Day

Bronze mask of drinking fountain in Main Entrance Hall. The mask is surrounded with fronds, fluttering ribbons, and a flower swag.

On the east side of the Main Entrance Hall, on the way to the Reading Room, the regularity of the arcade is interrupted by a portico of equal height, which does duty as a sort of miniature triumphal arch, commemorating the erection of the Library (see Plate V between pages 16 and 17). The spandrels contain two sculptured figures in marble by Olin Levi Warner, the sculptor of the bronze doors previously described. Along the frieze are the words "LIBRARY OF CONGRESS," inscribed in tall gilt letters. A second inscription, giving the names of those concerned in the erection of the Library, is cut upon the marble tablet which forms part of the parapet above. It is flanked by lictors' axes and eagles, sculptured in marble, and reads as follows:

ERECTED UNDER THE ACTS OF CONGRESS OF
APRIL 15 1886 OCTOBER 2 1888 AND MARCH 2 1889 BY
BRIG. GEN. THOS. LINCOLN CASEY
CHIEF OF ENGINEERS U. S. A.

BERNARD R. GREEN SUPT. AND ENGINEER
JOHN L. SMITHMEYER ARCHITECT
PAUL J. PELZ ARCHITECT
EDWARD PEARCE CASEY ARCHITECT

Warner's figures in the spandrels of this commemorative arch are life-size, and are entitled *The Students*. Both figures—one in either spandrel—are represented in an easy, but dignified and sculptural attitude, leaning on one arm against the curve of the arch. That to the left is of a young man seeking to acquire from books a knowledge of the experience of the past. That to the right is an old man with flowing beard, absorbed in meditation. He is no longer concerned so much with books as with observation of life and with original reflection and thought. The sculptor has thus naturally indicated the development of a scholar's mind, from youth to old age. As an ornament of the approach to the Reading Room, the appropriateness of the figures is obvious.

Olin Levi Warner's
Spandrel Figures

Within the arch, the pier on either side is decorated with a bit of relief work by Philip Martiny, consisting of the seal of the United States flanked by sea horses (left) and the torch of learning also with sea horses. It is Martiny's sculpture, also, which ornaments the staircase, the coved ceiling, and the lower spandrels of the Main Entrance Hall. With the exception of Warner's figures, just described, and of a series of cartouches and corner eagles which occupy the spandrels of the second-story arcade—the work of Weinert—Martiny has this central hall to himself, so far as the sculpture is concerned.

The spandrels in the first story are unusually delicate and pretty. The design comprises wreaths of roses and oak and laurel leaves, with oak or palm for a background. It is in the staircases, however, that Martiny's work is most varied and elaborate. On the piers between which they descend into the hall, he has sculptured a striking female head of the classic type, with a garland below and a kind of foliated arabesque on either side. Upon the newel post which terminates the railing of each staircase is placed a bronze female figure upholding a torch for electric lights. The two figures are somewhat taller than life, measuring 6½ feet, or 8 feet to the top of the torch, and 10 feet including the rounded bronze base on which they stand. Each has a laurel wreath about her head and is clad in classic drapery (see Plate VI between pages 16 and 17).

Philip Martiny's
Staircase Figures

Halfway up the staircase is a sort of buttress, which serves as a pedestal for a group representing, on the south side of the hall, Africa and America, and on the other side,

Two cherubs, America and Africa, with a globe and a bay leaf–bayberry swag at post on the Grand Staircase of the Main Entrance Hall. By Philip Martiny.

The railing of the south arm of the Grand Staircase of the Main Entrance Hall. Starting at the lower right, the cherubs represent a mechanic with cogwheel and pair of pincers, a hunter holding dead rabbit, a child Bacchus with champagne glass in left hand, and a farmer with sickle and sheaf of wheat.

Europe and Asia. The four continents are typified, very delightfully, by little boys, about 3 feet high, seated by the side of a large marble globe, on which appear the portions of the earth's surface which they are intended to personify. *America* is an Indian, with a tall headdress of feathers, a bow and arrow, and a wampum necklace. With one hand he shades his eyes while he gazes intently into the distance. *Africa* is a little Negro, with a war club and his necklace of wild beasts' claws. *Asia* is a Mongolian, dressed in flowing silk robes, the texture of which, as the visitor will notice, is very perfectly indicated by arranging the folds of the marble so that they receive the proper play of light and shade. In the background is a sort of dragon-shaped jar of porcelain. *Europe* is clad in the conventional classic costume, and has a lyre and a book; and an Ionic column is introduced beside him—the three objects symbolizing, specifically, Music, Literature, and Architecture.

Beneath *Asia* and *Europe* in a niche is the plaster bust of Thomas Jefferson and beneath *America* and *Africa* is the bronze bust of George Washington, both by the French sculptor Jean-Antoine Houdon.

The balustrade of the top landing on either side is ornamented with the figures of three children in relief representing certain of the fine arts. In the south staircase, beginning at the left as one looks up from the floor, are

At the north landing of the Grand Staircase of the Main Entrance Hall. Painting with palette and brushes, Architecture with compass and scroll, and Sculpture modeling a statuette. By Philip Martiny.

Comedy, Poetry, and *Tragedy.* The first has a comic mask and the thyrsus or ivy-wreathed wand of Bacchus, to whom the first comedies were dedicated. *Poetry* has a scroll, and *Tragedy* the tragic mask. Opposite, the figures, taking them again from left to right, are *Painting,* with palette and brushes; *Architecture,* with compasses and a scroll, and behind him the pediment of a Greek Temple; and *Sculpture,* modeling a statuette.

In the ascending railing of each staircase Martiny has introduced a series of eight marble figures in high relief. These, also, are of little boys, and represent various occupations, habits, and pursuits of modern life. The procession is bound together by a fruit garland hanging in heavy festoons, and beneath is a heavy laurel roll. In the center the series is interrupted by the group on the buttress just described. At the bottom it begins quaintly with the figure of a stork. Thence, on the south side of the hall, the list of subjects is as follows: a Mechanic with a cogwheel, a pair of pincers, and a crown of laurel, signifying the triumphs of invention; a Hunter, with his gun, holding up by the ears a rabbit which he has just shot; an infant Bacchanalian, with Bacchus's ivy and panther skin, hilariously holding a champagne glass in one hand; a Farmer, with a sickle and a sheaf of wheat; a Fisherman, with rod and reel, taking from his hook a fish which he has landed; a little Mars,

51

polishing a helmet; a Chemist, with a blowpipe; and a Cook, with a pot smoking hot from the fire.

In the north staircase are a Gardener, with spade and rake; an Entomologist, with a specimen box slung over his shoulder, running to catch a butterfly in his net; a Student, with a book in his hand and a mortarboard on his head; a Printer, with types, a press, and a type case; a Musician, with a lyre by his side, studying the pages of a music book; a Physician, grinding drugs in a mortar, with a retort beside him, and the serpent sacred to medicine; an Electrician, with a star of electric rays shining on his brow and a telephone receiver at his ear; and lastly, an Astronomer, with a telescope, and a globe encircled by the signs of the zodiac which he is measuring by the aid of a pair of compasses.

The Ceiling of the Main Entrance

Beneath the second-story cartouches on the east and west sides of the hall are tablets inscribed in gilt letters with the names of the following authors: Longfellow, Tennyson, Gibbon, Cooper, Scott, Hugo, Cervantes. A single molding in the marble cornice above is touched with gold, as an introduction to the rich coloring and profuse use of gilding in the coved ceiling which it supports. The cove itself is of stucco, and is painted blue—the color of the sky, which it is intended to suggest—with yellow penetrations. These penetrations are outlined by a heavy gilt molding, and give space for ten semicircular latticed windows opening into the rooms of the attic story. In the center of each penetration is painted a white tablet supported by dolphins, and bearing the name of some illustrious author—Dante, Homer, Milton, Bacon, Aristotle, Goethe, Shakespeare, Molière, Moses, and Herodotus. In each corner of the cove are two female half figures, as they are called, supporting a cartouche, on which are a lamp and a book, the conventional symbols of learning. The figures and cartouche are of stucco, and were modeled by Martiny (see Plate VII between pages 16 and 17). Around them the cove is sprinkled with stars. Higher up are the figures of flying cherubs, two in each corner, painted by Frederick C. Martin, of Garnsey's staff.

Between the penetrations, the curve of the cove is carried upon heavy gilt ribs, richly ornamented with bands of fruit. In the spandrel-shaped spaces thus formed on either side, Martin has painted another series of cherubs, which, by reason of the symbolic objects which accompany them, reflect very pleasantly the intention of Martiny's sculpture in the staircases below. The significance of most of the things they bear is obvious. Beginning at the southwest corner, and going to the right, the list is as follows: a pair of Panpipes; a pair of cymbals; a caduceus, or Mercury's staff; a bow and arrows; a shepherd's crook and pipes; a tambourine; a palette and brushes; a torch; a clay statuette and a sculptor's tool; a bundle of books; a triangle; a second pair of pipes; a lyre; a palm branch and wreath (the rewards of success); a trumpet; a guitar; a compass and block of paper (for Architecture); a censer (for Religion); another torch; and a scythe and hourglass—the attributes of Father Time.

The ceiling proper rests upon a white stylobate supported on the cove. It is divided by heavy beams, elaborately paneled, and ornamented with a profusion of gilding, and contains six large skylights, the design of which is a scale pattern, chiefly in blues and yellows, recalling the arrangement in the marble flooring beneath.

THE NORTH CORRIDOR–MAIN ENTRANCE HALL

The North, South, and East Corridors on the first floor of the Entrance Hall are paneled in Italian marble to the height of 11 feet, and have floors of white, blue, and brown (Italian, Vermont, and Tennessee) marble, and beautiful vaulted ceilings of marble mosaic. These last will immediately attract the attention of the visitor. The working cartoons were made by Herman T. Schladermundt from preliminary designs by Edward Pearce Casey as architect. The body of the design is in a light, warm grayish tone, relieved by richly ornamental bands of brown which follow pretty closely the architectural lines of the vaulting—springing from pier to pier or outlining the penetrations and pendentives. In all three corridors tablets bearing the names of distinguished men are introduced as part of the ornament, and in the East Corridor are a number of discs, about 18 inches in diameter, on which are depicted "trophies," as they are called, emblematic of various arts and sciences,

The Mosaic Vaults

53

Sample of mosaic vaulting to be found in the North, East, and South Corridors of the Main Entrance Hall. Cartoons by Herman T. Schladermundt under the supervision of Edward Pearce Casey.

each being made up of a group of representative objects such as the visitor has seen used to distinguish the subjects of Philip Martiny's staircase figures.

The method of making and setting such a mosaic ceiling is interesting enough to be described. The artist's cartoon is made full size and in the exact colors desired. The design, color and all, is carefully transferred by sections to thicker paper, which is then covered with a coating of thin glue. On this the workman carefully fits his material, laying each stone smooth side down. The ceiling itself is covered with a layer of cement, to which the mosaic is applied. The paper is then soaked off, and the design pounded in as evenly as possible, pointed off, and oiled. As the visitor may see, however, it is not polished, like a mosaic floor, but is left a little rough in order to give full value to the texture of the stone.

At the east end of the North and South Corridors is a large semi-elliptical lunette 22 feet long. Along the walls are smaller lunettes, below the penetrations of the vault. At the west end, over the arch of the window, is a semi-circular border. These spaces are occupied by a series of paintings—in the North Corridor by Charles Sprague Pearce, and in the South Corridor by Henry Oliver Walker. Like most of the special mural decorations in the Library, they are executed in oils on canvas, which is afterward affixed to the wall by a composition of white lead.

Charles Sprague Pearce's Paintings

Pearce's decorations are seven in number. The subject of the large tympanum at the east end is *The Family*. The smaller panels along the north wall, taking them from left

54

One of the panels in the North Corridor of the Main Entrance Hall, part of a series, "The Family," by Charles Sprague Pearce. This lunette on the west wall shows two female figures holding aloft a scroll with an inscription by Confucius.

Photo: The Library of Congress

to right, are entitled *Religion, Labor, Study,* and *Recreation.* The single painting on the south side of the corridor, occurring opposite the panel of *Recreation,* represents *Rest.* The broad, arched border at the west end contains two female figures floating in the air and holding between them

The North Corridor of the Main Entrance Hall looking east. The east lunette shows the hunter returning to his family from the chase, part of the series "The Family," by Charles Sprague Pearce.

Photo: Anne Day

a large scroll on which is inscribed the sentence, from Confucius: "Give instruction unto those who cannot procure it for themselves."

The series, as seen by the list of titles just given, illustrates the main phases of a pleasant and well-ordered life. The whole represents the kind of idyllic existence so often imagined by the poets—showing a people living in an Arcadian country in a state of primitive simplicity, but possessing the arts and habits of a refined cultivation. This life is very well summed up in the first of Pearce's paintings—that representing *The Family*. The subject is the return of the head of the household to his family, after a day spent in hunting. He stands in the center, his bow not yet unstrung, receiving a welcome home. His aged mother, with her hands clasped over the head of her staff, looks up from the rock on which she is sitting, and the gray-bearded father lays aside the scroll in which he has been reading. The hunter's little girl has hold of his garment, and his wife holds out his baby son. An older daughter leans her elbow against a tree. The scene is in the open air, at the mouth of a cave, with a view beyond into a wooded valley bounded by high mountains.

The smaller lunettes illustrate the simple occupations and relaxations of such an existence as is here depicted. *Recreation* shows two girls in a glade of the forest playing upon a pipe and a tambourine. In the panel of *Study,* a girl, sitting with her younger companion on a great rock, is instructing her with the aid of a book and compasses and paper. *Labor* is represented by two young men working in the fields. One is removing the stump of a tree, and the other is turning over the newly cleared soil to fit it for planting. In *Religion,* a young man and a girl are kneeling before a blazing altar constructed of two stones, one set upon the other. In *Rest,* two young women are sitting quietly beside a pool, where they have come with their earthen jars for water.

The penetrations in the vault of Pearce's corridor contain the names of men distinguished for their work in furthering the cause of education: Froebel, Pestalozzi, Comenius, Ascham, Howe, Gallaudet, Mann, Arnold, Spencer.

Religion, *with a man and woman worshiping. One of the panels in the North Corridor of the Main Entrance Hall devoted to "The Family," by Charles Sprague Pearce.*

Study *shows a young woman instructing another. One of the panels in the North Corridor–Main Entrance Hall, depicting "The Family," by Charles Sprague Pearce.*

THE LIBRARIAN'S ROOM (Visited Only by Permission)

Photo: Anne Day

One of four relief figures on the saucer dome of the Librarian's Room by Albert Weinert.

At the east end of the North Corridor of the Main Entrance Hall, beneath *The Family* a small door leads to the Librarian's Room. First comes the low-ceilinged secretary's office with the room proper beyond. It has a shallow dome, with stucco ornamentation in low relief by Albert Weinert. Standing in a ring around a central disc are the figures of Grecian girls, from two slightly differing models, holding a continuous garland. Other ornaments are gilded tablets and square or hexagonal panels, bearing an owl, a book, or an antique lamp. The central disc is occupied by a painting by Edward J. Holslag, already spoken of as the foreman of Elmer E. Garnsey's staff, representing *Letters*—the seated figure of a beautiful woman holding a scroll in her hand and accompanied by a child with a torch. The following Latin sentence is inscribed in a streamer: *"Litera scripta manet"* (The written word endures").

In the pendentives of the dome, Weinert has modeled a figure, about 2 feet in height, of a boy holding a palm branch and blowing a trumpet. Like the ring of girls in the dome, the figures are of an alternating design. Above each is a circular panel with the half-length figure of a woman, painted by Holslag. The four decorations are intended to supplement, in a general way, the idea of Holslag's ceiling disc; one of the figures, for example, holds a book, another a lute (for the musical quality of literature), and so on. Each painting contains a Latin inscription as follows: *"Liber dilectatio animae"* or ("Books, the delight of the soul"; *"Efficiunt clarum studio"* ("Study, the watchword of fame"; *"Dulce ante omnia Musae"* ("The Muses, above all things, delightful"; *"In tenebris lux"* ("In darkness light").

Two lunettes on the north and south sides of the room—broken by two bays with windows and two bays with doors—are pleasant studies of the evolution of the poet. At the bottom, a little boy is playing a pastoral tune on his oaten pipe; above, two little trumpeters blare at him to join them in the joy of battle; and at the top, a fourth child, the full-fledged bard, sits astride his modern hobbyhorse. The center of the decoration shows either a Pegasus or a Pandora, the latter opening the famous box containing all the ills which plague mankind, and only Hope for a blessing.

In the Librarian's Room. On a pendentive beneath the saucer dome a winged youth blowing a trumpet by Albert Weinert stands beneath a circular panel by Edward J. Holslag showing a young woman playing a lute. The Latin inscription, Dulce Ante Omnia Musae, *is translated* "The Muses, Above All Things, Delightful."

58

Photo: Anne Day

To the right of the entrance of the Librarian's Room, beneath Charles Sprague Pearce's *The Family,* is a roster of the Librarians of Congress:

John Beckley 1802–1807
Patrick Magruder 1807–1815
George Watterston 1815–1829
John Silva Meehan 1829–1861
John C. Stephenson 1861–1864
Ainsworth Rand Spofford 1864–1897
John Russell Young 1897–1899
Herbert Putnam 1899–1939
Archibald MacLeish 1939–1944
Luther Harris Evans 1945–1953
Lawrence Quincy Mumford 1954–1974
Daniel J. Boorstin 1975–

THE NORTH CORRIDOR AND THE NORTHWEST PAVILION

The North Corridor off the Librarian's Room (see Plate VIII between pages 16 and 17), at right angle to the North Corridor–Main Entrance Hall, looks out upon an interior court. The floor is of mosaic, and the walls are painted in simple tones of color with pilasters of white Vermont marble polished to a waxy surface. The ceiling is a succession of small domes in white and gold. In the center of each is a large gilt rosette. Around it are hexagonal coffers or panels ornamented with painted figures. The broad arches between (see Plate IX between pages 16 and 17) are decorated with coffers and panels in relief (see Plate X between pages 16 and 17), and the lunettes beneath (one at either end of the corridor, and seven along the west wall) are occupied with panels by Edward Simmons, representing the nine muses.

Edward Simmons's Paintings

The Muses, according to the Greek mythology, were the goddesses of the various departments of Art, Poetry, and Science. Apollo, the god of song, was their father, and Mnemosyne (Memory) their mother. Their names, given in the order in which they occur in Simmons's series, beginning at the south end of the corridor, were as follows: Melpomene, Clio, Thalia, Euterpe, Terpsichore,

Melpomene or Tragedy, one of the nine muses. The lunette by Edward Simmons is over the entrance to the North Corridor near the Librarian's Room.

Erato, Polyhymnia, Urania, and Calliope. Melpomene was the Muse of tragedy; Clio, of history; Thalia, of comedy and bucolic poetry; Euterpe, of lyric song; Terpsichore, of dancing; Erato, of erotic poetry; Polyhymnia, of sacred song; Urania, of astronomy; and Calliope, of epic poetry.

In Simmons's panels, each of the Muses is shown as a seated figure. On either side a laurel wreath is displayed, as the general symbol of intellectual pursuits, and the background is diversified by curving lines of smoke proceeding from the flame of a torch or a censer—thus signifying the inspiration of art and poetry. In several of the lunettes the Muse is accompanied by little cherubs who serve to bring out the special character of the central figure. In the panel devoted to Thalia the cherub is a satyr, with goat's legs, and carrying a pair of Panpipes. The Muse playfully catches him in a fold of her garment—the whole suggesting the rustic sportiveness of the early Greek comedy. Certain of the panels also contain various distinguishing objects. Melpomene, for example, is accompanied by a tragic mask; Clio by a helmet, for the warlike exploits recorded by history; Thalia, by a comic mask; Urania by a celestial globe. Terpsichore is represented as if swaying to the music of the dance and is striking a pair of cymbals. Erato is nude and bears a rose—the flower of love—in her hand. Polyhymnia holds an open book in her lap. One of the cherubs in the lunette of Calliope holds a scroll, and the other some peacock's feathers—the latter symbolical, perhaps, of the dignity and beauty of the epic.

Decorations by Robert Leftwich Dodge and W. Mills Thompson

At the end of this corridor is the Northwest Pavilion, decorated in a deep Pompeiian red with medallions containing figures of dancing girls by Robert Leftwich Dodge, and conventional ornaments adapted from Pompeiian designs. In the six window bays also is the series of the signs of the zodiac, designed by W. Mills Thompson.

THE EAST CORRIDOR–MAIN ENTRANCE HALL

The visitor retraces his steps to the Main Entrance Hall and goes east beneath the Commemorative Arch to the East Corridor.

John White Alexander's Paintings

In the East Corridor are six lunettes of the same size as the smaller panels of Pearce, by John White Alexander, illustrating *The Evolution of the Book*. The subjects are, at the south end, the Cairn, Oral Tradition, and Egyptian Hieroglyphics; and at the north end, Picture Writing, the Manuscript Book, and the Printing Press. In the first of these, a company of primitive men, clad in skins, are raising a heap of stones on the seashore, perhaps as a memorial of some dead comrade, or to commemorate some fortunate event, or, perhaps, merely as a record to let others know the stages of their journey. In the second panel, an Arabian storyteller stands relating his marvelous tales in the center of a circle of seated Arabs. The third shows a scaffolding swung in front of the portal of a newly erected Egyptian temple. A young Egyptian workman is cutting a hieroglyphic inscription over the door, while an Egyptian girl, his sweetheart, sits watching the work beside him. *Picture Writing* represents a young American Indian, with a rudely shaped saucer of red paint beside him, depicting some favorite story of his tribe upon a dressed and smoothed deerskin. An Indian girl lies near him, attentively following every stroke of his brush. The next panel gives the

62

A monk illuminating a manuscript, or The Manuscript Book, *one of six lunettes in the East Corridor by John White Alexander on "The Evolution of the Book."*

interior of a monastery cell, with a monk, seated in the feeble light of a small window, laboriously illuminating in bright colors the pages of a great folio book. The last of the series shows Gutenberg, the inventor of printing, in his office: the master, with his assistant beside him, examining a proof sheet, and discussing the principle of his great invention. To the right is an apprentice, swaying upon the handle bar of the rude press.

The Printing Press, *one of six lunettes in the East Corridor by John White Alexander devoted to "The Evolution of the Book." Gutenberg, the inventor of printing, is seen examining proof.*

Beneath the lunette *The Printing Press,* which depicts Gutenberg, is the following inscription:

THESE MEN OF THE
LIBRARY OF CONGRESS
CHARLES EDWIN CHAMBERS
EDWARD THEODORE COMEGYS
FRANK EDWARD DUNKIN
JOHN WOODBURY WHEELER
GAVE THEIR LIVES
IN THE
WORLD WAR
1918

Mosaic Decorations of the East Corridor

The various trophies already spoken of as ornamenting the mosaic of the vault of the East Corridor are ten in number, each occurring in one of the pendentives, at the ends and along the sides. Below each are the names of two Americans (only those actually born in the United States being included) eminent in the art or science typified. The list of trophies, with the names, is as follows: Architecture (the capital of an Ionic column, with a mallet and chisel), Latrobe and Walter; Natural Philosophy (a crucible and pair of balances, etc.), Cooke and Silliman; Music (a lyre, flute, horn, and music sheet), Mason and Gottschalk; Painting (a sketchbook, palette, and brushes), Stuart and Allston; Sculpture (the torso of a statue), Powers and Crawford; Astronomy (a celestial globe), Bond and Rittenhouse; Engineering (including an anchor, protractor, level, etc.), Francis and Stevens; Poetry (a youth bestriding Pegasus), Emerson and Holmes; Natural Science (a microscope and a sea horse), Say and Dana; Mathematics (a compass and counting frame), Peirce and Bowditch. In the vault proper is inscribed a list of names of Americans distinguished in the three learned professions: under Medicine, Cross, Wood, McDowell, Rush, Warren; under Theology, Brooks, Edwards, Mather, Channing, Beecher; and under Law, Curtis, Webster, Hamilton, Kent, Pinkney, Shaw, Taney, Marshall, Story, and Gibson.

THE LOBBIES OF THE ROTUNDA READING ROOM

Beyond the East Corridor, and separated from it by an arcade, is the passageway leading to the Reading Room. The Visitors Gallery, however, is by way of the second floor, the doors on the Reading Room floor being open only to those desiring to consult books. The passageway is divided by a second arcade into two transverse lobbies. The ceiling of each is vaulted, with a mosaic design like those in the corridors already described.

The second lobby is the immediate vestibule of the Reading Room, and contains the two main passenger elevators, one at either end.

The first lobby contains five lunettes, of the same size as Alexander's, which are filled by a series of paintings by Elihu Vedder, illustrating, in a single word, Government. Small as it is, the little lobby offers the painter one of the most significant opportunities in the whole interior; work here placed, in an apartment of the Library which serves at once as elevator hall and as vestibule to the Main Reading Room, can hardly fail to attract the attention of everyone passing through the building. It could not be more conspicuous anywhere outside the central Reading Room, and the selection of such a subject as Government is, therefore, peculiarly appropriate. In every sort of library the fundamental thing is the advancement of learning—illustrated in the Reading Room dome, as the visitor will see later—but in a library supported by the nation the idea of government certainly comes next in importance.

The painting in the central lunette, over the door leading into the Reading Room, is entitled simply *Government*. It represents the abstract conception of a republic as the ideal state, ideally presented. The other lunettes explain the practical working of government, and the results which follow a corrupt or a virtuous rule. The figures in these four lunettes are, therefore, appropriately conceived somewhat more realistically. The decoration to the left of the central lunette illustrates Corrupt Legislation, leading to Anarchy, as shown in the lunette at the end of the lobby, over the elevator. Similarly, on the other side, Good Administration leads to Peace and Prosperity. In all five, the composition consists of a central female figure, repre-

Elihu Vedder's Paintings

Photo: Anne Day

Bronze ornament above the elevator door in the second lobby or vestibule of the Rotunda Reading Room. Cartouche in scroll frame with bay-leaf wreath surrounded by rinceaux, egg-and-dart and bead-and-reel moldings, and two griffins.

senting the essential idea of the design, attended by two other figures which supplement and confirm this idea.

In the first painting, *Government,* the central figure is that of a grave and mature woman sitting on a marble seat or throne, which is supported on posts whose shape is intended to recall the antique voting urn—a symbol which recurs, either by suggestion or actually, in each of the other four lunettes. The meaning is, of course, that a democratic form of government depends for its safety upon the maintenance of a pure and inviolate ballot. The throne is extended on either side into a bench, which rests, at each end, upon a couchant lion, with a mooring ring in his mouth, signifying that the ship of state must be moored to strength. The goddess—for so, perhaps, she is to be considered—is crowned with a wreath, and holds in her left hand a golden scepter (the Golden Rule), by which the artist means to point out that no permanent good can accrue to a government by injuring another. With her right hand she supports a tablet inscribed with the words, from Lincoln's Gettysburg Address, "A government of the people, by the people, for the people." To the right and left stand winged youths, the first holding a bridle, which stands for the restraining influence of order, and the other with a sword with which to defend the State in time of danger, or, if one chooses, the sword of justice—it may be taken either way. The background of the group is the thick foliage of an oak tree, emblematic of strength and stability.

In the second panel, to the left, Corrupt Legislation is represented by a woman with a beautiful but depraved face sitting in an abandoned attitude on a throne the arms of which are cornucopias overflowing with the coin which is the revenue of the State. But this revenue is represented not as flowing outward, for the use and good of the people, but all directed toward the woman herself. The artist's idea was that when revenue is so abundant, as here depicted, that it greatly exceeds the needs of government, then government becomes a temptation to all kinds of corrupt practices. The path in front of the throne is disused and overgrown with weeds, showing that under such a corrupt government the people have abandoned a direct approach to Justice. With her right hand, the woman waves away, with a contemptuous gesture, a poorly clad girl—representing Labor—who comes, showing her empty distaff and spindle, in search of the work which should be hers by right, but which she cannot obtain under a government inattentive to the wrongs of the people. In her left hand the woman holds a sliding scale—used as being more easily susceptible of fraud than a pair of balances, and the proper emblem, therefore, of the sort of justice in which she deals. A rich man is placing in it a bag of gold; he sits confidently beside her, secure of her favors in return for his bribe. At his feet are other bags of gold and a strongbox, together with an overturned voting urn filled with ballots, signifying his corrupt control of the very sources of power. In his lap he holds the book of law, which he is skilled to pervert to his own ends. In the background are his factories, the smoke of their chimneys testifying to his prosperity. On the other side the factories are smokeless and idle, showing a strike or shutdown; and the earthen jar in which the savings of Labor have been hoarded lies broken at her feet.

The logical conclusion of such government is Anarchy. She is represented entirely nude, raving upon the ruins of the civilization she has destroyed. In one hand she holds the wine cup which makes her mad, and in the other the incendiary torch, formed of the scroll of learning. Serpents twist in her disheveled hair, and she tramples upon a scroll, a lyre, a Bible, and a book—the symbols, respectively, of Learning, Art, Religion, and Law. Beneath her feet are the dislocated portions of an arch. To the right, Violence, his eyes turned to gaze upon the cup of madness, is prying out the cornerstone of a temple. To the left, Ignorance, a female figure with dull, brutish face, is using a surveyor's staff to precipitate the wreckage of civilization into the chasm which opens in the foreground. Beyond, lying in an uncultivated field, are a broken millwheel and a millstone. But the end of such violence is clearly indicated; no sooner shall the cornerstone be pried from the wall than the temple will fall and crush the destroyers; and beside the great block on which Anarchy has placed her foot lies a bomb, with a lighted fuse attached. Such a condition, says the painting, must inevitably contain the seeds of its own destruction.

On the other side of the central lunette, Good Administration sits holding in her right hand a pair of scales evenly poised, and with her left laid upon a shield, quartered to

Good Administration, *by Elihu Vedder, depicts a woman with a pair of scales in her right hand. Nearby a young woman, Virtue, winnows wheat. To her left a young man, Intelligence, is voting by dropping his ballot into an urn. One of five panels in the lobby to the Rotunda Reading Room.*

represent the even balance of parties and classes which should obtain in a well-ordered democracy; on this shield are emblazoned, as emblems of a just government, the weight, scales, and rule. The frame of her chair is an arch, a form of construction in which every stone performs an equal service—in which no shirking can exist—and, therefore, peculiarly appropriate to typify the equal part which all should take in a democratic form of government. On the right is a youth who casts his ballot into an urn. He carries some books under his arm, showing that education should be the basis of the suffrage. To the left is another voting urn, into which a young girl is winnowing wheat, so that the good grains fall into its mouth while the chaff is scattered by the wind—an action symbolic of the care with which a people should choose its public servants. In the background is a field of wheat, a last touch in this picture of intelligence and virtue and, in itself, symbolic of prosperous and careful toil.

In the last panel, that of *Peace and Prosperity,* the central figure is crowned with olive, the emblem of peace, and holds in her hands olive wreaths to be bestowed as the reward of excellence. On either side is a youth, the one to her right typifying the Arts, and the other, Agriculture. The former sits upon an amphora or jar, and is engaged in decorating a piece of pottery; behind him is a lyre, for Music, and in the distance a little Grecian temple, for Architecture. The other is planting a sapling, an act suggestive of a tranquil, just, and permanent government, under which alone one could plant with any hope of enjoying the shade and fruit of afteryears. The background

68

of the picture is a well-wooded and fertile landscape, introduced for much the same purpose as the wheat field in the preceding lunette.

Still another piece of symbolism is expressed in this interesting series of pictures by the trees, their foliage forming the background against which the central figure is placed. The oak in the central panel has been spoken of. In the design representing Peace and Prosperity, an olive tree typifies not only Peace but Spring; in the next panel, that of *Good Administration,* the tree is the fig, and the season summer; in that of *Corrupt Legislation,* the autumnal vine, hinting at a too abundant luxury, and with its falling leaves presaging decay; and in that of *Anarchy,* bare branches and winter.

THE SOUTH CORRIDOR–MAIN ENTRANCE HALL

The South Corridor–Main Entrance Hall is, as mentioned above, a twin of the North Corridor–Main Entrance Hall except that it contains the work of Henry Oliver Walker.

The general subject of Walker's decorations is Lyric Poetry. Like Pearce's, in the corresponding position, the painting in the large lunette at the east end of the corridor sums up in a general way the subject of the whole series. The scene is a wood, with a vista beyond into a wide and open champagne. Down the center a brook comes tumbling and splashing over its rocky bed. Although wild, and thus suggestive, perhaps, of the inspiration of poetry, the landscape purposely has, as a whole, a touch of artfulness, hinting, therefore, at the formalities of meter and rhyme. The titles of the figures which enter into the composition—all, with one exception, those of women—are named in the conventional border with which the artist has enclosed his painting. The figure standing boldly forward in the center represents Lyric Poetry. She is crowned with a wreath of laurel and is touching the strings of a lyre. The feelings which most commonly inspire her song are personified on either side. To her left are Pathos, looking upward as if calling on Heaven to allay her grief; Truth, a beautiful nude woman (the Naked Truth) standing securely

Henry Oliver Walker's Paintings

Lyric Poetry, *is the theme of Henry Oliver Walker's panels in the South Corridor of the Main Entrance Hall. In the large lunette on the east wall Lyric Poetry with a lyre stands in the center while, starting on the left, are Mirth (boy), Beauty (seated woman), and Passion (woman with right arm held high), and, from the right, Devotion (seated woman), Truth (standing nude), and Pathos (woman staring upward).*

upright and seeming by her gesture to exhort the central figure not to exceed the bounds of natural feeling; and in the corner of the lunette, Devotion, sitting absorbed in contemplation. On the other side of the panel are Passion, with an eager look, and her arms thrown out in a movement at once graceful and enraptured; Beauty, sitting calmly self-contained; and Mirth, the naked figure of a little boy, inviting her to join his play.

On a marble panel beneath is the following inscription in gold letters:

THESE MEN OF THE LIBRARY OF CONGRESS
GAVE THEIR LIVES IN THE SECOND WORLD WAR

ARTHUR MORSE ANDERSEN	JAMES ALBERT GRANIER
MILLARD MACDONALD BENNETT	RICHARD LOEB
ALEXANDER TRIVIZ CHAVEZ	JOHN FRANCIS MULLANEY
JAMES GEIGER COXETTER, JR.	CHARLES BERNARD ROSSI
EDWARD HENRY EDENS	WALDO ERNEST SCHMITT
JOHN WILLIAMS ELL	LOUIE MAURICE SMITH
WILLIAM DAVID GILES	JAMES COMPTON SOPER
CHARLES WARREN VAN SCOYOC, JR.	

For the smaller lunettes, Walker has taken single youthful male figures suggested by various poems by English and American poets—on the south side of the corridor, Tennyson, Keats, Wordsworth, and Emerson, and on the north side, Milton and Shakespeare. Although not always from lyrics, the general spirit of the scene selected is invar-

70

iably lyrical. The first painting shows Ganymede upon the back of the eagle—the form taken by Jupiter when he brought the boy from his earthly home to be the cupbearer of the gods. The lines referred to are in Tennyson's "Palace of Art":

> Flushed Ganymede, his rosy thigh
> Half-buried in the Eagle's down,
> Sole as a flying star shot thro' the sky
> Above the pillar'd town.

The next panel represents Endymion, in Keats's poem of that name, lying asleep on Mount Latmos, with his lover, Diana, the Moon, shining down upon him. The painter, however, had no special passage of the poem in mind.

The third panel is based on Wordsworth's lines beginning, "There was a Boy." A boy is seated by the side of a lake the surface of which reflects the stars:

> There was a Boy; ye knew him well, ye cliffs
> And islands of Winander!—many a time,
> At evening, when the earliest stars began
> To move along the edges of the hills,
> Rising or setting, would he stand alone,
> Beneath the trees, or by the glimmering lake;
> And there, with fingers interwoven, both hands
> Pressed closely palm to palm and to his mouth
> Uplifted, he, as through an instrument,
> Blew mimic hootings to the silent owls,
> That they might answer him. . . .
> Then, sometimes, in that silence, while he hung
> Listening, a gentle shock of mild surprise
> Has carried far into his heart the voice
> Of mountain-torrents; or the visible scene

Photo: The Library of Congress

Ganymede being carried off by Jupiter in the form of an eagle. One of a series of panels in the South Corridor of the Main Entrance Hall on the subject of Lyric Poetry by Henry Oliver Walker.

71

Would enter unawares into his mind
With all its solemn imagery, its rocks,
Its woods, and that uncertain heaven received
Into the bosom of the steady lake.

For Emerson, Henry Oliver Walker has selected the poem of "Uriel," representing the angel retired in scorn from his companions, on account of the anger with which they have received his proposition:

Line in nature is not found;
Unit and universe are round;
In vain produced, all rays return;
Evil will bless, and ice will burn.

In the selection of this subject, Walker has commemorated Emerson in a very interesting personal way—for the poem was written soon after the famous Phi Beta Kappa oration of 1838, and is understood to voice Emerson's feelings regarding the storm of opposition which that address had called forth. To the right of it in a niche is the bust of the composer Stephen Collins Foster, 1826–1864, by Walker Hancock.

Milton is represented, to the left of the large lunette, by a scene out of the masque of *Comus*—the vile enchanter Comus (in the guise of a shepherd) entranced at hearing the song of the Lady. The words which he speaks in the poem, and which Walker seeks to illustrate in his painting, are as follows:

Can any mortal mixture of earth's mould
Breathe such divine enchanting ravishment?

In Shakespeare, the artist has gone to *Venus and Adonis,* showing the dead body of Adonis, killed by the boar, lying naked in the forest. The painting refers to no particular lines in the poem.

The broad border at the west end is occupied by an idyllic summer landscape containing three seated female figures and a youth—the two figures to the left, one of them caressing a lamb, representing the more joyful moods of lyric poetry, and the other two its more solemn feelings. At the top is a streamer, with the words, from Wordsworth:

The Poets, who on earth have made us heirs
Of truth and pure delight by heavenly lays!

In the mosaic of the vault are the names of lyric poets, six Americans occupying the penetrations on the north side: Longfellow, Lowell, Whittier, Bryant, Whitman, Poe; and the following foreign and ancient lyricists in the south penetrations and along the center of the vault: Browning, Shelley, Byron, Musset, Hugo, Heine, Theocritus, Pindar, Anacreon, Sappho, Catullus, Horace, Petrarch, Ronsard.

THE SOUTH CORRIDOR

The South Corridor, at right angle to the South Corridor–Main Entrance Hall, duplicates the North Corridor except that its panels have as theme The Greek Heroes, by Walter McEwen.

Walter McEwen's Paintings

The series is the work of Walter McEwen. The special subjects are incidents, as related in Greek mythology, in the lives of the following heroes, taking the paintings in order from north to south: Paris, Jason, Bellerophon, Orpheus, Perseus, Prometheus, Theseus, Achilles, and Hercules.

Paris, son of Priam, king of Troy, was brought up as a shepherd on Mount Ida. When a dispute arose among the three goddesses, Juno, Minerva, and Venus, as to who should possess a golden apple inscribed "To the fairest," which Eris (Strife) had flung in the midst of an assembly of the deities, Paris was selected by Jupiter to decide their quarrel. He awarded the apple to Venus, who promised him the most beautiful woman in the world to be his bride. Hearing of the charms of Helen, wife of Menelaus, king of Sparta, Paris sailed to Greece, and by the aid of Venus carried her away to Troy—thus provoking the expedition of the Grecian chiefs, and the ten years' siege of Troy. McEwen's painting shows Paris at the court of Sparta, conversing with Menelaus, while Helen sits listening beside her husband.

Pelias, king of Iolchos in Thessaly, was warned by the oracle to beware of his nephew Jason. He, therefore, sent him in search of the Golden Fleece. This had belonged to a ram which had miraculously carried Phryxus and Helle, a brother and sister in danger of their lives through the

73

Paris appearing before Helen and her husband, Menelaus, king of Sparta. Panel in the South Corridor by Walter McEwen.

cruelty of a stepmother, across the sea to Colchis. Here, when the ram died, Phryxus hung up its fleece in the grove of Mars, where it was guarded by a sleepless dragon. Jason accepted the quest and is here shown inviting the Grecian heroes to join in the voyage which he is to make to Colchis in the ship Argo—to enroll themselves in the famous band of the "Argonauts."

The third painting shows Bellerophon receiving from Minerva a golden bridle with which he may guide the winged horse Pegasus. The hero had incurred the dislike of his kinsman Proteus, king of Argos, who sent him with a sealed message to Iobates, king of Lycia. The message desired Iobates to cause Bellerophon to be slain. Being unwilling to do this directly, Iobates sent him to encounter the Chimera, a horrible monster, part lion, part goat, and part serpent, which was devastating his domains, and which had overpowered all who had ventured to attack it. By the help of Minerva and the winged horse, Bellerophon was successful.

Orpheus, who charmed with his song the rocks, the trees, the wild beasts, and even the infernal powers, incurred the wrath of Bacchus, whose divinity he refused to worship. Bacchus, therefore, inflamed his priestesses, the Maenads, or Bacchantes, against the poet, who was slain, as here represented by McEwen, in one of their orgies.

Perseus was the son of Jupiter and Danaë. Danaë's father had heard that his daughter's son would be the cause of his death. He, therefore, set the mother and child afloat in the

*Prometheus warning his brother Epi-
metheus not to accept Pandora and
her box from the gods. Panel in the
South Corridor by Walter McEwen.*

sea in a chest, which was safely cast upon the island of
Seriphos, the ruler of which was Polydectes. By the time
Perseus had grown to manhood, Polydectes had fallen
madly in love with Danaë, and, fearing lest Perseus should
be a bar to his passion, he ordered him to cut off the head
of the Gorgon Medusa, whose face turned to stone everyone who looked upon it. Assisted by Minerva, Perseus
succeeded in his adventure. Returning to Seriphos he found
Danaë persecuted by Polydectes, and, appearing at the palace of the king while he and his court were sitting at din-
ner, he drew the head of Medusa from his wallet and turned
the whole company into stone.

Prometheus is represented as warning his brother Epimetheus not to accept Pandora from the gods. Prometheus, who, with his brother, was the first of mankind,
had outwitted Jupiter in the matter of offering sacrifices;
Jupiter, in return, had withheld fire from earth. Prometheus, however, secured it by stealth from heaven, and
Jupiter in revenge formed Pandora, the first woman, and
sent her to become the bride of Epimetheus. Epimetheus
disregarded his brother's advice and took Pandora and with
her the fatal box, which, when opened, let loose a cloud
of evils to torment, with only delusive Hope to console,
mankind.

Theseus is directed by Minerva to leave Ariadne, who
sleeps beside him, and proceed to Athens alone. Athens
had been compelled for years to send an annual tribute of
youths and maidens to Minos, king of Crete, to be
devoured by the Minotaur, a savage monster, half bull,

75

half man, who was confined in a Labyrinth. Theseus voluntarily sailed on the tribute ship, and reaching Crete gained the love of the daughter of Minos, Ariadne, by whose aid he was enabled, after slaying the Minotaur, to find his way out of the Labyrinth. Returning, he bore Ariadne away with him but deserted her at the island of Naxos, as here depicted, at the command of Minerva. There she was found by Bacchus, who made her his bride.

Achilles, disguised as a maiden and living among the women in the court of Lycomedes, king of Scyros, is discovered by Ulysses. Thetis, the mother of Achilles, had been forewarned that her son would die an early death, as it turned out afterward that he did, being slain by Paris before the walls of Troy. She, therefore, dipped him, while still an infant, in the River Styx. He was thus made invulnerable in every part of his body except his heel, by which his mother had held him, and which, therefore, remained unaffected by the sacred water. To make assurance doubly sure, Thetis sent him to Lycomedes to be reared as a maiden, far from the dangers of war. When the Greeks were arming for the siege of Troy, the oracle informed them that without Achilles the city could never be taken. The crafty Ulysses was, therefore, sent in search of him. He arrived at the court of Lycomedes disguised as a peddler, bearing in his basket weapons of war and feminine trinkets. Showing these among the women, all were eager to examine the ornaments; Achilles clutched at the sword and shield, thus discovering himself immediately to the keen eye of Ulysses.

Hercules was sold as a slave by Mercury to Omphale, queen of Lydia. They became enamored of each other, and Hercules, to please her, wore female garments, and spun among the female slaves. The artist here exhibits him aiding the queen in her task.

THE COUNCIL OF SCHOLARS ROOM (Visited Only by Permission)

Walter McEwen's corridor opens directly into a richly decorated gallery, formerly serving as a special reading room for members of the House of Representatives and now reserved for privileged scholars. No apartment in the

Library is more lavishly and sumptuously ornamented. The floor is dark quartered oak; the walls have a dado of heavy oak paneling about 11 feet high; and the deep window arches are finished entirely in the same material. Above the dado the walls are covered with ochre cloth. The ceiling is beamed and paneled, and is finished in gold and colors, with painted decorations in the panels, and encrusted conventional ornament in cream white along the beams. Over the three doors are carved oak lunettes by Charles Henry Niehaus, comprising two different designs—the first a central cartouche bearing an owl, and supported on either side by the figure of e seated youth; the other, the American eagle flanked by two cherubs. At either end of the room is a magnificent mantel of Siena marble. Over the fireplace is a large mosaic panel by Frederick Dielman, representing, at one end of the room, *Law,* and at the other, *History.* Above is a heavy cornice supported on beautiful columns of pavonazzo marble, the general color of which is gray instead of yellow, but with a system of veining which agrees very well with that of the Siena. In the center of the cornice is a small cartouche, of green onyx in the mantel to the south, and of labradorite, or Labrador spar, in the other, the latter stone being remarkable for its exquisite gradations of deep peacock blue, continually changing with the light and the point from which it is seen.

Dielman's mosaic panels are of the same size and shape, each being 7½ feet wide and 3 feet 7 inches high. They were executed in Venice, which for generations has been celebrated for the delicacy, accurate coloring, and nicety of fitting of its mosaics. The process and methods used in this work are much the same as in the ordinary sorts of mosaic—such as would be required for a ceiling, for example—although, of course, the pieces, or tesserae, must be fitted with much greater care and patience, so that every piece may take its place in a perfect gradation of color. The work of the painter consisted in making full-size cartoons in the exact colors desired in the mosaic; from these the Italian workmen prepared the finished panels, and sent them to this country ready to be put in place. The cartoons, however, were necessarily painted as much as possible in simple outlines and shades of color, for, although the Italian shops are said to have at their command enamels

Frederick Dielman's Mosaics

77

of no less than 25,000 different tints, it would be obviously impossible with such a material to reproduce exactly every variatfion of tone and line of which the brush is capable. Certain refinements of technique, therefore, and more especially the vagueness of color which is often so desirable in the painted canvas, must be avoided in a cartoon made for such a purpose as Dielman's.

The mosaic at the north end of the room represents Law, typified by a young and beautiful woman seated on a massive marble throne and holding in one hand a sword with which to chastise the guilty, and in the other a palm branch with which to reward the meritorious. Her head is surrounded by a glory, and she wears on her breast the aegis of Minerva to signify that she is clad in the armor of righteousness and wisdom. On the steps of her throne are the scales of Justice and the book of Law, and a pair of white doves emblematic of mercy. The visitor will notice that Dielman's conception of Law includes the conventional typification of Justice, but at the same time slightly differs from it. The reason is that he has wished to indicate not only the judicial but the legislative side of Law; hence the freer air of command and, in particular, the outdoor landscape of woods and hills, signifying a less restricted authority than that of the courtroom. Such a typical symbol of Justice as the scales is less conspicuously introduced, and the usual globe is entirely omitted.

To one side of the central throne are three figures representing, as one may see by the names in the streamer above them, respectively Industry, Peace, and Truth, the friends and supporters of Law; while on the other Dielman introduces three other figures typifying Fraud, Discord, and Violence, the enemies of Law. Industry and Violence are represented as male figures; the other four as female. Very appropriately, the first group seems to be advancing unafraid toward the throne of the goddess; while the figures to the right shrink terrified from her presence. The emblems which distinguish the various figures are easily understood: Industry with a wheel and hammer; Peace with an olive branch and crown of olive; Truth with the lilies; Fraud, represented as a withered hag; Discord, with disordered hair and garment, and holding a pair of knotted serpents; and Violence, in a steel cap with the blazing torch lying on the ground before him.

Dielman's second panel represents History. The titular figure, that of a woman of great charm and beauty, stands in the center holding a pen and a book. On either side are marble tablets bearing the names of great historians—Herodotus, Thucydides, Polybius, Livy, Tacitus, Baeda, Comines, Hume, Gibbon, Niebuhr, Guizot, Ranke, Bancroft, Motley. At the foot of one tablet is a laurel wreath, for peace, and on the other side an oak wreath, for war—the twin topics of history—each accompanied by a palm branch, the general reward of success. On either side of the panel extends a marble bench on which are seated two female figures representing Mythology and Tradition, the predecessors of history. Mythology, the expounder of the ancient tales of the gods and heroes, stands for theories of the system of the universe, in token of which she holds in her right hand a globe of the earth. Beside her is a sphinx—the female sphinx of the Greeks, not the male sphinx of Egypt—suggesting the eternally insoluble Riddle of the World. At the other end of the panel, Tradition, an aged granddame, relates her old wives' tales to the boy who sits listening before her. The figure represents the whole body of medieval legend and folk tale. Reminders of a past age are brought out in the distaff she holds in her lap, the Romanesque capital on which the boy sits, the harp he holds in his hand—with its reference to the wandering minstrel of the Middle Ages and his store of tales—and in

History holding a pen and a book with Mythology at her right hand and at her left, Tradition, a mature woman, and a boy. Mosaic by Frederick Dielman in the Council of Scholars Reading Room.

79

the shield, very likely the text of the story which is being told, which leans against the tablet.

In the background of the panel, seeming to float amidst the clouds, are three ancient buildings, an Egyptian pyramid, a Greek temple, and a Roman amphitheater—signifying the three nations of antiquity in which history was most highly developed.

Carl Gutherz's Paintings Along the center of the ceiling are seven panels containing decorations by Carl Gutherz, representing the Spectrum of Light. Each of the seven colors shown in the spectrum is typified by a central figure standing for some phase of achievement, human or divine. Other features of the panel are two cherubs in each corner, representing arts or sciences, and a series of eight escutcheons, one with the title of the decoration, and the other containing the seals of the various states, the whole being combined in a single arabesque pattern by an elaborate design of scroll ornamentation.

The order of the subjects begins in the center and goes first north and then south from that point. The color of the center panel is Yellow, and the subject the Creation of Light. The Divine Intelligence, sitting enthroned in the midst of Space, and enveloped in mist and clouds, utters the words, "Let there be Light." The corner figures represent Physics, Metaphysics, Psychology, and Theology.

The second color is Orange, and the subject the Light of Excellence, suggested to the artist by Longfellow's poem, "Excelsior." A spirit stands midway on a pyramid of steps (signifying Progress), which is lost in the unknown distance. She beckons to man to join her on the heights where she is standing, and holds in one hand the wreath which crowns every effort for Excellence. In the corner, the cherubs typify Architecture and Sculpture; Transportation; the Phonograph and Telephone; and Invention and Design.

The third panel is Red, representing the Light of Poetry. Poetry, mounted upon Pegasus, holds a torch in one hand and with the other reaches toward that light of the ideal for which he must always strive, but which he can never attain. In the background half-seen figures represent the afterglow of Tradition and Mythology. The corner groups stand for Tragedy and Comedy; Lyric Poetry; Pastoral Poetry; and Fable.

The Light of State, *one of seven panels devoted to "The Spectrum of Light" by Carl Gutherz. On the ceiling of the Council of Scholars Room.*

Violet, the fourth color, is symbolized as the Light of State. The United States being regarded as the highest form of government yet achieved, its emblems are selected as the best expression of the ideal state. This being the case, violet was the color under which, according to the conception of the artist, the United States might best be represented, since violet results from the union of the American colors, red, white, and blue. The figure is that of Columbia, with a shield emblazoned with the United States flag, and carrying a staff surmounted by a liberty cap, while the American eagle hovers above her shoulder. The cherubs in the corners represent the Suffrage, Justice, Liberty, and Equality.

The next subject is Green, or the Light of Research. The central figure is the Spirit of the Lens, which in the telescope and the microscope reveals to the scientist the secrets of the universe. She is surrounded by the sea, with its myriad forms of life furnishing her with the material for her investigations. The cherubs in one corner have a microscope. In another, they represent Chemistry; in the third Archaeology (Egyptology deciphering the hieroglyphics);

81

and in the fourth, Mineralogy—all selected as being especially concerned with original investigation and research.

Blue is the Light of Truth. The Spirit of Truth crushes the dragon of Ignorance and Falsehood underfoot, and reaches to heaven for a ray of light with which to inflict the final wound. The blue of the background is the blue of daylight—light from darkness. The cherubs hold the level, the plumb, and the Bible, each considered as an agent in indicating the presence of a universal law.

The last panel represents Indigo as the Light of Science. The figure represents Astronomy, who is guided by the soul (figured as a butterfly fluttering above her head) to explore the movement of the stars. The cherubs represent various phases of astronomical study. One of the figures, for example, explains the theory of mathematics, showing on the fingers of the hand that *one* is the unit of everything; a second looks through a telescope; and others are studying books and making calculations.

THE JEFFERSON CONGRESSIONAL READING ROOM
(Visited Only by Permission)

At the end of the corridor leading to the Jefferson Congressional Reading Room, originally reserved for senators, now used by all members of Congress and their staffs, is a little lobby, from which one enters the Southwest Pavilion, reserved for the use of members. The little lobby itself is one of the most beautiful examples of pure architectural design to be found in the Library. The walls are of Vermont marble—the same as in the corridor—paneled with Siena marble. The molded ceiling is finished entirely in gold, with a central rosette, surrounded by coffers and conventional Greek moldings, one of which, a rather elaborate fret, is laid upon a ground of deep red. The whole effect of the decoration, taken in connection with the low light which prevails, is remarkably fine—a combination of great richness with soberness and refinement.

The room is finished in much the same style as the Council of Scholars Room, but with less elaboration of ornament. On the whole, the effect, though quieter, is perhaps more restful and satisfying. A toilet room, leading

from the lobby just spoken of, cuts off a portion of the pavilion, but allows space above for a low gallery enclosed by a delicately carved balustrade of Siena marble. Below, the oak dado is ornamented with delicate inlaid arabesques of white mahogany. Above the dado the walls are covered with watered red silk. In the southwest corner is a fireplace of Siena marble, with a sculptured panel of the same material by Herbert Adams. The design shows an eagle with arrows in his claws, and an American shield supported by flying cherubs. The doorhead lunette is of oak, like those in the Council of Scholars Room, and contains a curved panel, also by Adams, with a heraldic shield bearing the monogram "U.S.A." and supported by mermaids. The gold ceiling contains six square panels, each containing four graceful female figures holding garlands in their hands—the work of William A. Mackay.

TO THE VISITORS' GALLERY OF THE ROTUNDA READING ROOM

Returning again to the Main Entrance Hall the visitor takes one of the two Grand Staircases to the beautifully decorated corridors of the second-story arcades in order to reach the public gallery of the Main Reading Room in the Rotunda.

The vaulting of the broad passageway leading to the

83

Visitors' Gallery consists of a series of six small domes. The colors are light and bright, and the three different patterns employed consist mainly of garlands and ribbons, and of simple bands of color radiating from a central medallion. Swans, eagles, or owls are introduced both in the domes and as the ornament of the pendentives, and eagles occur between the double consoles which receive the weight of the domes upon the east wall. In the medallions just referred to are various objects symbolizing the Fine Arts—tragic and comic masks, for Acting; a lyre, for Music; a block of marble, half shaped into a bust, and sculptors' tools, for Sculpture; a lamp, scrolls, and an open book, for Literature; and the capital of an Ionic column, a triangle, and some sheets of parchment, for Architecture.

The trophies of Sculpture and Architecture, it should be added, are accompanied by appropriate names—comprising those of cities, statues, and buildings—inscribed both in the arabesques and in the pendentives of certain of the domes. For Architecture, the buildings commemmorated are the Colosseum, the Taj Mahal, the Parthenon, and the Pyramids; while the cities are those with whose fame these four great monuments are connected—Rome, Agra, Athens, and Gizeh. The sculptures are the Farnese Bull, the Laocoön, the Niobe, and the Parthenon pediment, and in the bordering arabesques are the names of the four divinities often taken as the subject of ancient statuary—Venus, Apollo, Hercules, and Zeus.

In the center of the passage a marble staircase, dividing to the right and left at a landing halfway up, leads to the gallery of the Rotunda. Beneath, on either side, are little bays giving access to the elevators. In the decoration of the ceiling the effect aimed at is that of an arbor, with a grapevine, climbing over a trellis, painted against a sunny yellow background. Each contains a small lunette, the right one depicting William Hickling Prescott and the left one John James Audubon. (They replaced panels by William B. Van Ingen.)

The visitor returns to the foot of the staircase and proceeds to the landing.

Elihu Vedder's Mosaic Decoration

The wall of the landing of the staircase is occupied by an arched panel, 15½ feet high and 9 feet wide, containing a marble mosaic by Elihu Vedder. (see Plate XI between pages

16 and 17) The artist has chosen for his subject Minerva, her armor partly laid aside, appearing as the guardian of civilization. She is the Minerva of Peace, but Vedder indicates that the prosperity which she now cherishes has been attained only through just and righteous war, whether waged against a foreign enemy or against the forces of disorder and corruption within. Beside her is a little statue of Victory, such as the Greeks were accustomed to erect in commemoration of their success in battle. The figure is that of a winged woman standing on a globe, and holding out the laurel wreath and palm branch to the victors. In the sky the clouds of disaster and discouragement are rolled away and about to disappear, while the sun of reappearing prosperity sends its rays into every quarter of the land. Although her shield and helmet have been laid upon the ground, the goddess still retains the aegis and holds in one hand, like a staff, her long, two-headed spear, showing that she never relaxes her vigilance against the enemies of the country which she protects. For the present, however, her attention is all directed to an unfolded scroll which she holds in her hand. On this is written a list of various departments of learning, science, and art, such as Law, Statistics, Sociology, Botany, Bibliography, Mechanics, Philosophy, Zoology, etc. To the left of Minerva is the owl, perched upon the post of a low parapet. Olive trees, symbolizing peace, grow in the field beyond. The armor of the goddess is carefully studied from ancient sculptures. The character of the aegis can here be more easily made out than in any of the other representations of Minerva to be found in the building. Traditionally a cape of goatskin, the Greek artists finally came to overlay it with metal scales, like scale armor. The border is composed of twisting serpents. The head of the Gorgon Medusa, which forms the central ornament, is used also as the decoration of the large shield lying in the foreground of the picture. The helmet is decorated with a pair of rams' heads. Vedder's whole design is surrounded by a border containing, on either side, a conventionalized laurel tree displayed like a vine. Beneath the mosaic is the inscription, *Nil invita Minerva, quae monumentum aere perennius exegit,* Not unwilling, Minerva raises a monument more lasting than brass, from Horace, *Ars Poetica.*

85

Entering by either of the doors at the head of the staircase, the visitor at once steps out upon an embayed gallery, affording a spacious and uninterrupted view of the great domed Rotunda Reading Room, which, in every sense, is the central and most important portion of the Library. As such, it is marked by a magnificence of architecture and decoration nowhere else to be found in the building. Richer materials have been used, and decoration has been more freely employed than in any other part of the Library (see Plate XII between pages 16 and 17). Sculpture and paintings, rare marbles, and a broad scheme of color and of ornamentation in stucco relief unite with a lofty architectural design to form what is one of the most notable interiors in the country.

The Importance of the Rotunda

The detailed description of the Rotunda may be deferred a little, however, in order to explain its relation to the rest of the building and, especially, the reason for its central position. Besides accumulating books and providing the student with proper accommodations for his or her work—such as good light and convenient chairs and tables—it is the business of every well-managed library to supply its readers with the books they desire in the shortest possible time and with the least possible amount of friction. A well-digested catalogue is the first requisite; the second is that the books should be stored in a place as closely accessible to the reading room as may be. In a small library this is a simple matter; the same room will be sufficient for both books and readers. When the number of volumes increases, it is necessary to shelve them in a compact system of bookcases called a "stack"—or, as in the Library of Congress, in a series of stacks—which must occupy a portion of the building by itself. The reading room and the stacks being thus separated, it is still the aim of the architect to place them in such a way as to retain as far as possible the practical convenience of the smaller library, where every reader is almost within reaching distance of every book. This end is most easily attained by adopting what is called the "central system" of library construction, which is the system followed in the Library of Congress. It has already been seen that the building is in the form of a cross enclosed within a rectangle, thus allowing space for four courts for light and air. At the intersections of the arms of the cross is the Rotunda, the main entrance to which is through the west arm of the cross. The other three arms are occupied by the stacks; the East Stack, directly opposite, is the second short arm; the North and South Stacks, each the same length, are the two long arms. It is obvious that by this arrangement the books can be more easily reached than in any other way. The axes of the stacks are continued radii of the Rotunda, and, so far as the ground plan is concerned, the shortest way from any part of the cross to the Issue Desk which the visitor sees below in the center of the room is always along a straight line. This Issue Desk, of course, being in the exact center of everything, is the vital point, the kernel, of the whole arrangement. No part of the stack, it will be noted, is far enough away from it to delay the transmission of a book unreasonably, as might very well be the case if the three stacks were in one.

Another thing may well be noted in this connection although it has already been referred to in the preliminary description of the building—and that is the comparative unimportance, from the standpoint of the real requirements of the Library, of the rectangle which encloses the stacks and the Rotunda, as necessarily appears from the street to be the main portion of the building. It contains rooms which, at present, are very convenient for clerical work or as art galleries and special reading rooms, and which may in time be necessary to accommodate an overflow of books; but it must steadily be borne in mind that the Rotunda and the stacks contain the real life of the institution. They are the only really essential and vital portion of the building; without them, there could hardly be a library; and by themselves they would be sufficient for almost every present need.

The character of the Rotunda is warm and rich in ornament as befits a room where people remain to read. It is naturally not so formal as the Rotunda of the Capitol. The height of the room from the floor to the top of the dome, where it converges upon the lantern, is 125 feet, and from the floor to the crown of the domed ceiling of the lantern itself, 160 feet. This latter point, however, is quite shut off from the view of a person standing in the gallery and can

The General Arrangement

87

be seen only from a position near the center of the room. The ground plan of the room is octagonal in shape, measuring 100 feet from one side to another. Eight massive clustered piers, each set some 10 feet forward from a corner of the octagon, support a series of heavy arches running entirely round the room. These piers serve, as it were, to stake out the limit of the Reading Room proper; between them are marble screens arcaded in two stories, and behind they are connected with the outer wall by partitions which divide the octagon into eight bays or alcoves, each 14 feet deep and 30 wide.

The alcoves are arched and enclose great semicircular windows filled with stained glass, which furnish the greater part of the light needed for the room. The arches springing

Looking southeast from the Visitors' Gallery across the Rotunda Reading Room. A high engaged Corinthian column is set against a cluster of Corinthian pilasters rising from a high base. Above is a broken entablature from which spring the arches of the great bays and a pendentive rising to the dome. The statue representing Art holds a model of the Parthenon. It is the work of François Tonetti-Dozzi, based on sketches by Augustus Saint-Gaudens.

from the piers support a heavy circular entabulature, immediately above which is the dome, arched in the line of an exact circle and supported upon eight ribs dividing it into eight sections or compartments. The ribs are the essential feature of the dome construction, and continue naturally the line of support of the great piers which are the ultimate support of the whole interior—a fact which is more clearly brought out to the eye by paired consoles or brackets introduced in the entablature between the two and seeming to carry the weight from one to the other.

The surface of the dome is of stucco, attached to a framework of iron and steel filled in with terra cotta, and richly ornamented with coffers and with a very elaborate arabesque of figures in relief. At the top, where the dome prepares to join the lantern, the ribs terminate against a broad circular "collar," so called, containing a painted decoration by Edwin Howland Blashfield. Finally comes the lantern, 35 feet in height, and pierced by eight windows, recalling the octagonal arrangement with which the construction began. The shallow dome which covers the lantern is ornamented with a second painting by Blashfield, summing up the idea of his decoration in the collar.

At the risk of some tediousness, perhaps, but thinking that afterward the connection between the decoration and the architecture would be more clearly understood, the writer has given this general description of the Rotunda, in order that the visitor might immediately see what portion of the whole was essential and what not essential; what was "structural" and vital, in other words, and what not. It will have been observed that we have, on the outside, an octagon supporting a shallow dome, on which rests the lantern. Well within this is an octagonal arrangement of piers carrying a much steeper dome. Alcoves occupy the space between the inner and outer octagons. Between the two domes—the inner shell and the outer—is vacancy. The whole exterior—walls, dome, and lantern—the partitions back of the piers, and the connecting screens, all could be torn away and the inner dome still remain secure on its eight massive piers.

The piers are constructed of brick, veneered with marble from Algeria, curiously mottled and in color a sort of dusky red. The high base on which the pier rests is sheathed with a chocolate-brown variety of the familiar close-grained

Tennessee marble. The height of the piers, including base and capital, is 44 feet.

The screens are built solidly of marble from Siena, Italy, which encloses in its rich black veining almost every variety of yellow, from cream color to dark topaz. Like the piers, the screens are erected upon a Tennessee marble base, in this case, however, very much lower—4 feet to the other's 11. The arcading of the screens is in two stories, the first of three and the second of seven arches. At the top of each screen the gallery is railed in by a heavy balustrade—still of the same Siena marble—connected with which are two marble pedestals which bear bronze statues of illustrious men. The screens are alike on every side of the octagon but two, the west and the east—the former the entrance from the Main Entrance Hall, and the latter affording a way through to the east side of the building. In both instances, therefore, the central arch is accentuated by free-standing columns. In the second story of the west screen, also, still another modification has been made in order to allow space for a large clock—the three middle arches giving place to a rich architectural setting ornamented with bronze statuary.

The Alcoves   The alcoves behind the screens are in two stories, like the arcading, and are intended to contain a collection of the most necessary standard books on all important topics. The entrance from the floor of the Reading Room is through the central arch of the screen. One may pass through doors in the partitions from one alcove to another, on either floor; and by means of a winding staircase inside each of the piers one may go up or down, not only from story to story, but into the basement below and to the space between the inner and the outer dome above.

In front of each of the great piers of the Rotunda is an engaged column (see Plate XIII between pages 16 and 17), so called because it is not quite clear of the mass behind it, which serves as the ultimate support of a statue placed between the arches upholding the dome. In height, base, and capital, it is the same as the pier with which it is connected and, like it, is sheathed in Algerian marble, but not so dark in tone, since the burden resting on the column includes no part of the dome and is, therefore, much lighter than that borne by the pier.

The engaged columns, however, join with the piers to carry an elaborate entablature some 7 feet in height, which, finding its way in and out of the alcoves from pier to pier, completely encompasses the room. The color of the entablature, which is entirely of stucco, is a cream or ivory white, like the dome, touched sparingly with gold. The moldings, which are of the usual Roman patterns employed in Renaissance architecture, are very rich and heavy. The topmost member of the cornice is boldly projected upon a series of modillions, the soffits between being ornamented with rosetted coffers—gilt on a blue ground. The frieze is enriched with an arabesque of Renaissance ornament in relief, including antique urns and lamps; garlands enclosing tablets; and winged half figures. The general design of the frieze, as of all such work in the Library, is by Edward Pearce Casey as architect; the individual figures, however, were modeled by Albert Weinert.

Portion of the main frieze of the Rotunda Reading Room showing flaming urns and winged figures ending in acanthus leaves. The frieze relief was designed by Edward Pearce Casey, while the figures were executed by Albert Weinert.

The Symbolic Statues

The eight statues set upon the entablature over the engaged columns represent eight characteristic features of civilized life and thought. From the floor to the plinth or base on which they stand is a distance of 58 feet; each is 10½ feet, or, including the plinth, 11 feet high. All are of plaster, toned an ivory white to match the general tone of the stucco decoration throughout the room, and are effectively placed against the plain red pendentives of the dome as a background. The title of each is inscribed in gilt letters in a tablet in the frieze below. Beginning with the figure directly to the right as one enters the west gallery of the Rotunda, the order is as follows: *Religion,* modeled by Theodore Baur; *Commerce,* by John Flanagan; *History,* by Daniel Chester French; *Art;* by François M. L. Tonetti-Dozzi, after sketches by Augustus Saint-Gaudens; *Philosophy,* by Bela Lyon Pratt, who modeled the granite spandrels of the Main Entrance; *Poetry,* by John Quincy Adams Ward; *Law,* by Paul Wayland Bartlett; and *Science,* by John Donoghue.

Nearly all bear some appropriate and distinguishing object. Religion holds a flower in her hand, seeming to draw from it the lesson of a God revealed in Nature. Commerce, crowned with a wreath of the peaceful olive, holds in her right hand a model of a Yankee schooner and in her left a miniature locomotive. History has a book in her hand,

Commerce, holding a sailing ship and steam locomotive, stands on the entablature at the base of a pendentive in the Rotunda Reading Room. John Flanagan, sculptor.

Law, with a scroll in her left hand, her right hand resting on the Tablet of the Law, stands on the entablature at the base of a pendentive in the Rotunda Reading Room. Paul Wayland Bartlett, sculptor.

and with an obvious symbolism holds up a hand glass so that it will reflect thing behind her. Art is unlike the other figures in being represented as nearly nude. She is crowned with laurel, and bears a model of the Parthenon. Beside her is a low tree, in the branches of which are hung a sculptor's mallet and the palette and brush of the painter. Philosophy is a grave figure with downcast eyes, carrying a book in her hand. The garment of Poetry falls in severe lines, which suggest the epic and the more serious forms of the drama, rather than the lighter aspects of the Muse. Law has a scroll in her hand; a fold of her robe is drawn over her head to signify the solemnity of her mission; and beside her is the stone Tablet of the Law. Science holds in her left hand a globe of the earth, surmounted by a triangle. In her right hand is a mirror, not, like History's, turned backward, but held forward so that all may perceive the image of Truth.

Above each statue the pendentive of the dome is occupied by a group in plaster, sculptured by Philip Martiny, consisting of two winged figures, modeled as if half-flying, half-supported on the curve of the arches, and holding between them a large tablet carrying an inscription in gilt letters. Above the tablet is a pair of crossed palm branches (meaning peace), and below are the lamp and open book symbolic of learning, these last being surrounded by an oak wreath, typifying strength—the whole group thus signifying the power and beneficence of wisdom.

The inscriptions were selected by President Eliot of Harvard University, who several years before had furnished the memorable sentences carved upon the Water Gate at the World's Columbian Exposition of 1893 in Chicago. Each is appropriate to the subject of the statue below it.

Thus, above the figure of Religion are the words:

> What doth the Lord require of thee, but to do justly, and to love mercy, and to walk humbly with thy God?
> —Micah 6:8

Above the figure of Commerce:

> We taste the spices of Arabia yet never feel the scorching sun which brings them forth.
> —Dudley North

Above the figure of History:

One God, one law, one element,
And one far-off divine event,
To which the whole creation moves.   —Tennyson

Above the figure of Art:

As one lamp lights another, nor grows less,
So nobleness enkindleth nobleness.   —Lowell

Above the figure of Philosophy:

The inquiry, knowledge, and belief of truth is the
sovereign good of human nature.   —Bacon

Above the figure of Poetry:

Hither, as to their fountain, other stars
Repairing, in their golden urns draw light. —Milton

Above the figure of Law:

Of law there can be no less acknowledged than that
her voice is the harmony of the world.   —Hooker

Above the figure of Science:

The heavens declare the glory of God; and the
firmament sheweth his handiwork.   —Psalms 19:1

The sixteen bronze statues set along the balustrade of the *The Portrait Statues*
galleries represent men illustrious in the various forms of
thought and activity typified in the figures just described.
The arrangement of the statues is in pairs, each pair flanking one of the eight great piers of the Rotunda. The list of
those who have been thus selected to stand as typical representatives of human development and civilization is as
follows: Under *Religion,* Moses and Saint Paul; *Commerce,*
Columbus and Robert Fulton; *History,* Herodotus and
Gibbon; *Art,* Michelangelo (a single figure, but standing
at once for Architecture, Sculpture, and Painting) and Beethoven; *Philosophy,* Plato and Lord Bacon; *Poetry,* Homer
and Shakespeare; *Law,* Solon and Chancellor Kent (the
author of the well-known *Commentaries*); *Science,* Newton
and Professor Joseph Henry. The sculptors were: of the
Moses and *Gibbon,* Charles H. Niehaus; *Saint Paul,* John
Donoghue (the sculptor of the figure of *Science*); *Columbus*
and *Michelangelo,* Paul Wayland Bartlett (who modeled the
figure of *Law*); *Fulton,* Edward Clark Potter; *Herodotus,*
Daniel Chester French (*History*); *Beethoven,* Theodore Baur
(*Religion*); *Plato* and *Bacon,* John Joseph Boyle; *Homer,* Louis

93

Sir Isaac Newton representing Science, by Cyrus Edwin Dallin.

Sir Francis Bacon representing Philosophy, by Joseph Boyle.

Professor Joseph Henry, secretary of the Smithsonian Institution, representing Science.

William Shakespeare, representing Poetry, by Frederick MacMonnies.

Saint-Gaudens; *Shakespeare,* Frederick MacMonnies (who did the central doors at the Main Entrance); *Solon,* Frederick Wellington Ruckstull (the sculptor of the busts of Goethe, Macaulay, and Franklin, in the Entrance Portico); *Kent,* George Bissell; *Newton,* Cyrus Edwin Dallin; and *Henry,* Herbert Adams, whom the visitor already knows for his work in connection with Olin Levi Warner on the bronze entrance doors, as well as for his little figures of Minerva in the Main Vestibule.

Of these figures, two, the *Moses* and *St. Paul,* are ideal, though modeled, in a general way, according to conventions long established in Christian art. The *Solon* is an original study, although, of course, aiming to be entirely Greek in spirit and costume. The *Homer* follows an ancient ideal bust. The *Herodotus* and *Plato* are studied from original Greek sculptures. The features of the other ten are taken from portraits from life, and the costumes are accurately copied from contemporary fashions.

The *Moses* of Niehaus holds the Table of the Law, and, like Michelangelo's famous figure, is horned—a curious convention which crept into art from an ancient mistran-

Herodotus as a traveler, representing History, by Daniel Chester French.

Chancellor Kent of New York, representing Law, by George Edwin Bissell.

Robert Fulton with a steamboat, representing Commerce, by Edward Clark Potter.

slation of a passage in Exodus. The *Saint Paul* is a bearded figure, one hand on the hilt of a great two-edged sword, and the other holding a scroll. Ruckstull has conceived his *Solon* as the typical lawgiver of the ancient world. He is represented as stepping forward, clothed in all the power of the state, to announce at a solemn gathering of the people the supremacy of Law over Force. A fold of his garment is drawn over his head with a certain priestly suggestion, as if the laws he proclaimed were of divine origin. He holds aloft, in his left hand, a scroll bearing the Greek words *"OI NOMOI,"* which, though meaning simply "The Law," were understood as referring especially to Solon's enactments. His right hand rests upon a sheathed and inverted sword, which is wreathed with laurel. The idea is that law has supplanted force, but that force is always ready to carry out the mandates of the law. *Homer* is represented with a staff in his hand and a wreath of laurel crowning his head. French represents *Herodotus* as a traveler, searching the known world for the materials of his histories. His garments are girt up, he bears a long staff in one hand, and shades his eyes with a scroll as he gazes into

Plato, representing Philosophy, by Joseph Boyle.

Photos: The Library of Congress

the distance to discover his destination. The *Fulton* carries a model of a steamboat, and the *Henry* an electromagnet, for discoveries in electrical science. The *Beethoven* shows the composer with his hand uplifted as if to beat the measure of the harmony which has suddenly come into his mind—so suddenly that in the eagerness of his movement he has pulled the pocket of his greatcoat inside out. MacMonnies's *Shakespeare* is a somewhat novel study so far as the head is concerned; it is a composite of the portrait in the first collected edition of the plays and of the Stratford bust. The figure of *Kent* wears the judicial ermine; he carries in one hand the manuscript of his *Commentaries,* and holds a pen in the other. Of the other figures, some, like the *Gibbon,* carry a book or pen; but in most instances the sculptor has sought merely to give his subject an appropriately noble and contemplative attitude and expression, without trying to introduce any special symbol of his work.

John Flanagan's Clock Still another piece of sculpture—the group ornamenting the great clock over the entrance to the Rotunda—remains to be spoken of before passing on to a description of the dome and Blashfield's decorations. It is the work of John Flanagan, the sculptor of the figure of Commerce, and, taken altogether, is one of the most sumptuous and magnificent pieces of decoration in the Library. The clock itself is constructed of various brilliantly colored precious marbles, and is set against a background of mosaic, on which are displayed, encircling the clock, the signs of the zodiac, in bronze. Above is a life-size figure, executed in high relief in bronze, of Father Time, striding forward, scythe in hand. To the left and right are the figures of maidens with children, also in bronze, representing the Seasons. The dial of the clock is about 4 feet in diameter; in the center is a gilt glory, or "sunburst." The hands, which are also gilded, are jeweled with semiprecious stones.

Including, of course, Weinert's and Martiny's work, it will be seen that no less than nineteen American sculptors have contributed to the decoration of the Rotunda. Considering the room—just for the moment, and for the sake of the special point of view—merely as a gallery of statuary, it will be seen how important and representative a collection of American sculpture has been brought together. The choosing of the sculptors to be commissioned, and of

the work to be assigned to each—not only here but throughout the Library—were necessarily matters of very careful consideration. To aid in this work, General Casey secured the advice of the president of the National Sculpture Society, John Quincy Adams Ward, who associated with him as a committee two others of the most prominent members of the society, Augustus Saint-Gaudens and Olin Levi Warner. This committee went into the question very thoroughly and, as a result, recommended the sculptors for the Entrance Portico, the bronze entrance doors, the Commemorative Arch in the Main Entrance Hall, and the Rotunda. Their advice was accepted *in toto,* with the result, barring a few changes made necessary by subsequent circumstances, that the visitor has now seen.

The soffits of the arches upholding the dome are ornamented with a row of plain coffers; the larger arches which roof the alcoves within, carry a triple row of more elaborate coffers, each with a gilt rosette. The windows of stained glass, already spoken of as enclosed by these arches,

The Rotunda clock with the figure of Father Time and his scythe, by John Flanagan. Over the main entrance to the Rotunda Reading Room.

The Lighting of the Rotunda

97

are semicircular in form and measure 32 feet across at the base. They furnish the greater part of the light needed for the illumination of the room. No shadows are cast in any direction. Being so high above the floor, the light from them is much more effective than if they were nearer the level of the reader's eye. They are better even than skylights, and with none of the disadvantages of skylights. Other sources of light are the various little windows pierced in the four walls of the Octagon which face the interior courts; and, above, the eight windows of the Lantern. Edwin Howland Blashfield's paintings in the dome, for example, can hardly be said to receive direct light from a single window in the room, but for all that, so perfectly is the light diffused, they are as easily made out as any decorations in the building.

The Semicircular Windows It is calculated that, by putting stained glass in the eight semicircular windows, the amount of light admitted has been diminished almost exactly one-eighth; in other words, the result is the same as if one of the eight had been quite closed up.

The cartoons for the stained glass were made by Herman T. Schladermundt after designs prepared by the architect, Edward Pearce Casey. The ground is a crackled white, leaded throughout into small, square panes. In order to give an effect of boldness and strength, the windows are divided vertically by heavy iron bars. The design is surrounded by a richly colored border of laurel, combined with rosettes and Roman fasces. At the top, in the middle of each window, is the great seal of the United States, 4 feet high, surmounted by the American eagle, whose outstretched wings measure 8 feet from tip to tip. To the right and left, following the curve of the window, are the seals of the states and territories, three on a side, or six in each window, so that forty-eight—excluding only Alaska and Indian Territory (Alaska became a state in 1959, and Indian Territory, along with the territory of Oklahoma, became the state of Oklahoma in 1907.)—are contained in the eight windows. Torches alternate with the seals, and the fasces are introduced at the bottom.

The name of the state or territory is inscribed above each seal, with the date of the year in which it was admitted to the Union or organized under a territorial form of govern-

98

ment. The seals occur in the order of their dates, the series beginning with the thirteen original states—which start in the easterly window in the order in which they signed the Constitution—and continuing around the room to the three territories of New Mexico, Arizona, and Oklahoma. (They did not achieve statehood until 1912, 1912, and 1907 respectively.) Taken all in all, they form one of the most interesting decorations in the Library, for the reason that the artist has succeeded in making a harmonious whole out of a very heterogeneous collection of designs. The originals, of course, were separately drawn, often by persons unacquainted with heraldry, and never with any particular thought of fitting them into a single series like the present. The result is that these originals show the greatest diversity of treatment. The key, so to speak, is continually changing. Sometimes, for example, a figure introduced in the foreground is dwarfed by an altogether disproportionate background, while in other cases the figure overpowers everything else; copied exactly, any heraldic or artistic unity of effect would be entirely lacking. Accordingly, after getting together a complete collection of the seals—in every instance an authentic impression of the original obtained from the state secretary—Schladermundt redrew, and often almost redesigned his material to bring it into accordance with his decorative scheme. Just what it was that Schladermundt undertook to do may best be seen in the accompanying engravings of the seal of Kansas, the first giving the seal as used on official papers, the second copied from Schladermundt's cartoon. It will be seen that the spirit of the seal and its heraldic intention are the same in both. The only difference is that in Schladermundt's design certain changes of proportion have been made to make the seal harmonize with the style to which the artist wished to have all his designs adhere. In many cases, particularly in the seals of the thirteen original states, the original had hardly been changed at all. In the seal of the state of Washington, indeed, which consists merely of a portrait of Washington himself, Schladermundt has unobtrusively added the Washington arms in the upper corner of the design, in order to suggest the desirable heraldic conventionality more fully; occasionally, too, it has been necessary to omit certain minor details as being unsuited to the breadth of treatment necessary in stained glass—but, as a

The seals of Washington and Kansas on the top and bottom as drawn by Herman T. Schladermundt for the windows of the Rotunda Reading Room. His Kansas seal on the bottom should be compared to the authorized seal of the state as shown in the center.

View of the top gallery of the Rotunda Reading Room showing three of the bronze statues on the balustrade and the statue of History above the entablature. Note the great seal of the United States and the state and territory seals in the windows.

Photo: Anne Day

Photo: Anne Day

Two female figures by Philip Martiny support an elaborate cartouche with scrolls above the keystone of one of the great arches of the Rotunda Reading Room.

rule, Schladermundt has followed very carefully the specifications contained in the authoritative legislative enactments.

A vertical section of the dome of the Rotunda would show an exact half circle, with a diameter of 100 feet. As has been said before, the dome is of stucco, applied to a framework of iron and steel, filled in with terra cotta. Although, as previously described, it appears to rest upon the deep upper entablature, it really springs immediately from the eight arches resting upon the great piers. The entablature, as will be seen on a close inspection, bears no part in the construction. It is projected so far forward from the dome that one may easily walk between the two.

The Dome

The entablature is about 7 feet high, with a richly molded architrave and a heavy projecting cornice. The ground of the frieze is gilt, with a relief ornament in white of eagles standing upon hemispheres and holding in their beaks a heavy garland of laurel. Over the north, south, east, and west arches, are two female figures—the work of Philip Martiny—represented as seated upon the architrave molding and supporting a heavy cartouche—another instance of the emphasis which the architect has so often placed upon the four main axes of the building.

The dome is so simply planned that a description of its main features may be given in a very brief space. The surface is filled with a system of square coffers. The ornamentation of the body of the dome is in arabesque. The eight ribs which mark off the dome into compartments are each divided into two by a band of gilded ornament resembling a guilloche. The coffers diminish in size from 4½ feet square at the bottom to 2½ feet at the top. The total number of coffers is three hundred and twenty—or forty in each compartment, and also in each horizontal row, and eight in each vertical row. The ground of the coffers is blue, the sky color, as if one were really looking out into the open air—and, therefore, the color traditionally used in coffering. To give sparkle and brilliancy, many shades and kinds of blue are used, the darker and heavier at the bottom, and the lighter and airier toward the top. The transition is so gradual and natural that the eye does not perceive any definite change, but only a generally increased

The Stucco Ornamentation

Cherub with winged torch standing in a bay-leaf wreath atop a vase. An ornamental panel of the Rotunda Reading Room dome by Albert Weinert.

vividness. The border moldings of the coffers are cream-colored—old ivory is the usual term—strongly touched with gold, and in the center of each is a great gold rosette.

Although the purpose of the dome arabesque is primarily to give an agreeable impression of light and shade, the individual figures of which it is composed are nearly as interesting a study as the general effect of the whole. The variety of the figures is almost bewildering—lions' heads, sea horses, dolphins, urns, cartouches, griffins, shells, storks, caryatids, tridents, eagles, cherubs, half figures, genii—altogether something like forty-five principal type designs, interwoven with very many smaller but no less beautiful pieces of ornament. All are adapted from Renaissance models of the best period, and are combined with the utmost spirit and harmony in an arabesque whose every portion has equal artistic value. No single figure catches the eye; broad horizontal and vertical bands of decoration, gradually diminishing as they approach the top, encircle and ascend the dome, each with its particular "note" of arrangement and design, but all cunningly united to form an indisputable whole, everywhere balanced and restrained.

Edwin Howland Blashfield's Paintings

The position of Blashfield's decorations in the collar and lantern of the dome is the noblest and most inspiring in the Library (see Plate XIV between pages 16 and 17). They are literally and obviously the crowning glory of the building and put the final touch of completion on the whole decorative scheme of the interior. The visitor will see how, without them, not a painting in the building would seem to remain solidly and easily in its place, for they occupy not only the highest, but the exact central point off the Library, to which, in a sense, every other is merely relative.

Tripod and two winged half-figures emerging from acanthus leaves. An ornamental panel of the Rotunda Reading Room dome by Albert Weinert.

As was hinted in the description of Elihu Vedder's paintings, Blashfield was almost necessarily drawn to select some such subject as he has here chosen—the Evolution of Civilization, the records of which it is the function of a great library to gather and preserve.

The ceiling of the lantern is sky and air, against which, as a background, floats the beautiful female figure representing the Human Understanding, lifting her veil and looking upward from Finite Intellectual Achievement (typified in the circle of figures in the collar) to that which is beyond; in a word, Intellectual Progress looking upward

Section of the Rotunda Reading Room dome showing the coffering with rosettes set in elaborately ornamented panels. Executed by Albert Weinert.

103

and forward. She is attended by two cherubs. One holds the book of wisdom and knowledge; the other seems, by his gesture, to be encouraging those beneath to persist in their struggle toward perfection.

The decoration of the collar consists of a ring of twelve seated figures, male and female, ranged against a wall of mosaic patterning. They are of colossal size, measuring, as they sit, about 10 feet in height. They represent the twelve countries, or epochs, which have contributed most to the development of present-day civilization in this country.

Straight-up view of the dome showing the diminishing size of the coffers and the way it was divided. The mural collar by Edwin Howland Blashfield is at the top. The hole in the center, black in the photograph, is filled with the same painter's The Human Understanding.

Human Understanding lifting her veil with two cherubs in attendance. The round mural set inside the lantern of the dome. Edwin Howland Blashfield, painter.

Photo: Anne Day

Beside each is a tablet, decorated with palms, on which is inscribed the name of the country typified, and below this, on a continuous banderole or streamer, is the name of some chief or typical contribution of that country to the sum of human excellence. The figures follow each other in chronological order, beginning, appropriately enough, at the East, the East being the cradle of civilization. The list is as follows: *Egypt,* typifying Written Records; *Judea,* Religion; *Greece,* Philosophy; *Rome,* Administration; *Islam,* Physics; *The Middle Ages,* Modern Languages; *Italy,* the Fine Arts; *Germany,* the Art of Printing; *Spain,* Discovery; *England,* Literature; *France,* Emancipation; and *America,* Science (see Plate XV between pages 16 and 17).

Each figure is winged, as representing an ideal, but the wings, which overlap each other regularly throughout, serve mainly to unite the composition in a continuous whole, and in no case have been allowed to hamper the artist in his effort to make each figure the picture of a living, breathing man or woman. Four of the twelve figures, it will be observed, stand out more conspicuously than the rest on account of the lighter tone of their drapery—*Egypt, Rome, Italy,* and *England.* They occupy, respectively the east, south, west, and north points in the decoration, and furnish another instance of the stress that has been laid, throughout the Library, upon the four cardinal points of the compass which govern the axial lines of the building, and which in turn have been enriched and dignified in the final decorative scheme of the interior. Each of these axial figures is painted in a more rigid attitude than those beside it, and forms, as will be noticed, the center of a triad, or group of three, each of the flanking figures leaning more or less obviously toward it. It should be noted that there was no intention on the part of the painter to magnify the importance of the four figures thus represented over any of the others. The emphasis of color is solely for decorative purposes. The arrangement being chronological, Blashfield was unable to exercise much control over the order in which each figure should occur, and still retain his original selection of countries.

Egypt is represented by a male figure clad in the loincloth and cap with lappets so familiar in the ancient monuments. The idea of Written Records is brought out by the tablet he supports with his left hand, on which is inscribed

Photo: Anne Day

in hieroglyphics the cartouche or personal seal of Mena, the first recorded Egyptian king, and by the case of books at his feet, which is filled with manuscript rolls of papyrus, the Egyptian paper. Besides the idea of Writing and Recording, Blashfield brings out the fact that the Egyptians were among the first who held the doctrine of the immortality of the soul. The figure holds in the right hand the Tau, or cross with a ring head, the emblem of life both in this world and beyond it; and on the tablet behind his feet in the winged ball, the more familiar symbol of the same idea.

The collar of the dome of the Rotunda Reading Room by Edwin Howland Blashfield. Twelve figures, about 10 feet in height, although seated, represent twelve nations or epochs that have contributed most to the development of America.

107

Judea is shown as a woman lifting her hands in an ecstatic prayer to Jehovah. The overgarment which she wears falls partly away, and discloses the ephod, which was a vestment worn by the high priests, ornamented with a jeweled breastplate and with onyx shoulder clasps set in gold, on which were engraved the names of the Twelve Tribes of Israel. On the face of a stone pillar set beside her is inscribed, in Hebrew characters, the injunction, as found in Leviticus 19:18—"Thou shalt love thy neighbor as thyself"—a sentence selected as being perhaps the noblest single text contributed by the Jewish religion to the system of modern morality. In her lap is a scroll, containing, presumably, a portion of the Scriptures; and at her feet is a censer, typical of the Hebrew ritualism.

The figure of Greece is distinctly suggestive, so far as attitude and drapery are concerned, of one of the beautiful little Tanagra figures of terra cotta—so called from the ancient Greek town in which they were first discovered—which are so familiar to students of Greek art. A bronze lamp is set beside her, and in her lap is a scroll—the emblems of wisdom. Her head is crowned with a diadem—possibly with a reference to the City of the Violet Crown, Athens, and Mother of Philosophy.

Rome, the second axial figure, wears the armor of a centurion, or captain in a legion. A lion's skin, the mark of a standard-bearer, is thrown over him, the head covering the top of his casque. The whole conception is that of the just but inexorable administration of Rome founded upon the power of its arms. One foot is planted upon the lower drum of a marble column, signifying stability. His right arm rests upon the fasces, or bundle of rods, the typical emblem of the Roman power and rule. In his right hand he holds the baton of command.

Islam is an Arab, standing for the Moorish race which introduced into Europe not only an improved science of Physics, as here used by Blashfield in its older and less restricted sense—but of mathematics and astronomy also. His foot rests upon a glass retort, and he is turning over the leaves of a book of mathematical calculations.

By the term *Middle Ages,* represented by the female figure which comes next in the decoration, is usually understood the epoch beginning with the dissolution of the Western Roman Empire in 455 and ending with the dis-

Photo: Anne Day

Portion of the collar of the dome by Edwin Howland Blashfield. Spain is shown as an explorer with a globe beside him and a caravel at his feet. England in Elizabethan dress holds a Shakespeare folio on her lap. France, seated on a cannon, holds in her left hand a scroll with the words "Les Droits de l'Homme."

covery of America in 1492. No single country is here indicated, for Europe was throughout that period in a state of flux, so to say, in the movement of which the principal modern languages were finally evolved from the Latin and Teutonic tongues. But it was an epoch notable for many other things, also. The figure typifying the epoch is distinguished by an expression at once grave and passionate, and has a sword, casque, and cuirass, emblematic of the great institution of Chivalry; a model of a cathedral, standing for Gothic Architecture, which was brought to its greatest perfection in these thousand years; and a papal tiara and the keys of Saint Peter, signifying medieval devotion and the power of the Church.

The next figure, Italy—the Italy of the Renaissance—is shown with symbols of four of the Fine Arts which she represents—Painting, Sculpture, Architecture, and Music. She holds a palette in her left hand, and with the brush in her right seems about to lay another stroke of color on her canvas. To her left is a statuette after Michelangelo's celebrated *David,* in Florence. At her feet is a Renaissance capital; and leaning against the wall a violin, at once the typical musical instrument and in the manufacture of which the Italians peculiarly excelled.

Germany is the printer, turning from his press—a hand press, accurately copied from early models—to examine the proof-sheet he has just pulled. His right foot is placed upon a pile of sheets already corrected, and a roller for inking lies convenient to his hand.

Spain is the sixteenth-century Spanish adventurer. He wears a steel morion on his head, and is clad in a leather jerkin. Holding the tiller of a ship in his right hand, he

109

seems to be watching for land to appear in the sea. Beside him is a globe of the earth, and at his feet a model of a caravel, the sort of ship in which Columbus sailed on his voyages, is introduced.

England wears the ruff and full sleeves of the time of Elizabeth—the era when English literature, both poetry and prose, was at its highest. She is crowned with laurel—the reward of literature—and bears in her lap an open book of Shakespeare's plays—the righthand page with a facsimile of the title page of the first edition of *A Midsummer Night's Dream,* dated 1600.

France, standing for Emancipation and the great revolutionary upheaval of the eighteenth century, is dressed in a characteristic garb of the First Republic—a jacket with lapels, a tricolor scarf, and a liberty cap with a tricolor cockade. She sits on a cannon and carries a drum, a bugle, and a sword—emblems of her military crusade in behalf of liberty. In her left hand she displays a scroll bearing the words "Les Droits de l'Homme," the famous Declaration of the Rights of Man adopted by the French Assembly in 1789.

The twelfth and last figure, bringing us once more round to the east, is that of America—represented as an engineer, in the garb of the machine shop, sitting lost in thought over a problem of mechanics he has encountered. He leans his chin upon the palm of one hand, while the other holds the scientific book which he has been consulting. In front of him is an electric dynamo—recalling the part which the United States has taken in the advancement of electrical science.

On the base of the dynamo, Blashfield has signed his work in an inscription which recalls also the name of the artist who assisted him in laying it upon the plaster: "These decorations were designed and executed by Edwin Howland Blashfield, assisted by Arthur Reginald Willett, A. D. MDCCCLXXXXI."

The visitor will perhaps have been a little perplexed by the familiar appearance of some of the faces in Blashfield's decoration. It is an interesting fact that in several cases he has introduced a resemblance, more or less distinct, to the features of some real person in order to give greater variety, and, above all, greater vitality to his figures. The persons chosen were selected because the character of their features seemed to him peculiarly suited to the type which he wished to represent. In the case of Abraham Lincoln—the figure of America—and of General Casey—Germany—the choice was fitting for other reasons. Among the female figures, the Middle Ages, is Mrs. De Navarro (Mary Anderson), and *England,* Ellen Terry, the English actress. The faces of Italy and Spain are from sketches made from Amy Rose, a young sculptor in New York, and William Bailey Faxon, the painter, respectively. France suggests the features of the artist's wife. Throughout, however, it must be remembered that, to use Blashfield's own words, "no portraiture has been attempted, but only characterization."

One can hardly leave this description of the decoration of the Rotunda without a word respecting the general color scheme. Beginning with the brown, red, and yellow marbles at the base, one ends with the pure whites and bright greens and violets of Blashfield's final decoration. The difference between these two extremes has been bridged over by the use of harmonizing colors on the walls and in the dome. The Pompeiian red of the alcove walls and the pendentives is suggested by the Algerian marble of the piers. A touch of brown on the wall below the semicircular windows echoes the brown Tennessee base, and the yellow predominant in the alcove arches above derives from the Siena screens. These last, again, in their lightest portions, strike the key for the "old ivory"—the delicate gray-yellow—which, either deeper or lighter, is always the ruling tone of the entablature, the dome, and the sculptural figures in plaster. The coffers of the dome, one will notice by looking closely, are defined by a narrow band of yellow or red—yellow throughout one whole compartment, and red in the next. The former carries up (more markedly than in the ivory-toned stucco) the color of the screens; the latter the color of the piers. The blue ground, moreover, and the yellow stripe create together, whether one will or not, an impression of green upon the eye, because green is compounded of blue and yellow; and the blue and the red, in turn, create an impression of violet, for a similar reason. Thus, the visitor, glancing up to the decorations of the collar, is already prepared for Blashfield's two dominating tones. The white is expected as the natural result of a color

The Rotunda Color Scheme

111

scheme which has been steadily growing lighter from the beginning, and, after being used in Blashfield's painting, it is at last appropriately employed almost solely in the lantern which crowns the whole Rotunda. Finally, considering the room as a whole, it will be noted that the profuse use of gold throughout the dome and lantern is not only legitimately suggested by the Siena marble, but of itself helps to keep the various colors—in marble or stucco—in what may be called a more complete "state of solution" than would otherwise have been possible. By attracting attention to itself, it softens the contrasts between the other colors.

THE SECOND-FLOOR CORRIDORS

Returning to the corridor above and between the Grand Staircases, the visitor may continue his or her tour of the Library by exploring the second-floor corridors. They are arranged like those on the first floor, but their greater height and the brighter tone of decoration give an effect of considerably greater spaciousness.

The Decoration of the Vaults   The floors of the corridors are laid in mosaic of varying patterns. The ceilings are uniformly a barrel vault, with pendentives—the same, that is, as those of the North, East, and South Corridors below. The vaults are covered with a painted decoration of Renaissance ornament which for variety and interest is hardly surpassed anywhere else in the building. The decorative scheme which has been adopted was planned throughout by Edward Pearce Casey, and elaborated, especially in the matter of color, and carried into effect, by Elmer Ellsworth Garnsey, working under Casey's direction.

Particular attention should be given the decoration as it is uncommon in this country. The younger Casey and Garnsey deserve special credit for having so much executed here and elsewhere in the Library.

In addition, each corridor contains, as a distinctive accent of color and design, a series of paintings by a specially commissioned artist—in the West Corridor by Walter Shirlaw, in the North Corridor by Robert Reid, in the East

Corridor by George Randolph Barse, Jr., and in the South Corridor by Frank Weston Benson. In the side corridors also, at the west end, the arch of the vault is spanned by a broad band of stucco ornament containing a series of octagonal coffers, ornamented in relief by Roland Hinton Perry.

The decoration is varied, of course, from corridor to corridor, in order to prevent any monotony of impression,

A sample of the elaborate decoration of the vaulting in the second-floor corridors. This, with the printer's mark of François Estienne, is in the South Corridor. The general scheme was fixed by Edward Pearce Casey and elaborated and executed under the supervision of Elmer Ellsworth Garnsey.

Photo: Anne Day

The printers' marks of William Caxton (North Corridor), Geoffroy Tory (South Corridor), and Melchior Lotter (West Corridor) On the second floor.

but the main principles on which it is based are everywhere the same. Thus the color scheme—which was suggested in part by the beautiful Piccolomini Library in Siena—comprises in every corridor blue in the pendentives, golden yellow in the penetrations, and a grayish white in the body of the vault. The only exception to this rule is in the West and East Corridors, which are terminated by double arches instead of ending directly upon a wall. Here the end penetrations are red and the pendentive yellow. The others remain as before. The delineation of the spaces is at bottom very simple, and though more elaborate, a good deal like that already noted in describing the mosaic in the lower corridors. The penetrations are outlined by a bright colored border, on which, where the lines converge to a point at the top, rests a border of greater width, enclosing the entire vault in a single great rectangle. This, in turn, is divided into compartments by bands of ornament, varying in number according to the requirements of the decoration, but always occurring immediately over the columns of the arcade. These bands, coming where they do, perform a vital service for the decoration in continually reminding the visitor, if only by a painted arabesque, of the importance of the arch in such a piece of construction as a vault. In the spaces between them are garlands and wreaths, and panels for paintings and inscriptions— the whole making part of one great arabesque, which is as easily intelligible and coherent as it is various, but which would have been bewildering in its wealth of ornament and color if it had not been for the fundamental service performed by these various bands and borders and broad masses of color.

The penetrations and pendentives are richly embellished with a great variety of ornament, both conventional and otherwise. The treatment differs in different corridors, however, on account of the varying relative position of the paired columns which support the arcade—from which results first a series of wide and then a series of narrow pendentives. Where the former occur—in the West and East Corridors—they are ornamented with the decorations of Shirlaw and Barse; while the narrower pendentives on the north and south carry simple medallions and tablets, and Reid's and Benson's paintings find place in the arabesque of the ceiling vault and in circular frames along the wall beneath. The balance is restored, however, by introducing a series of medallions, corresponding to Benson's and Reid's, though smaller and of less importance, in the vaults east and west, and by ornamenting the penetrations in the side corridors with greater richness and elaboration.

The most interesting decoration of the penetrations, however, is a series of "Printers' Marks" which is continued through all four corridors. Altogether there are fifty-six of them—sixteen in each of the side corridors, ten in the West Corridor, and fourteen in the East Corridor. They are painted in black outline, and are of a sufficient size, averaging about a foot and a half in height, to be easily made out from the floor. By a printer's mark, it should be explained, is meant the engraved device which the old printers used in the title page or colophon of their books, partly as a kind of informal trademark guarding against counterfeited editions, and partly as a personal emblem, such as a publisher of good standing would like to see on a long list of worthy books. For this latter reason, and in order to be able to add an interesting piece of ornament to the title page, the mark has been revived of late years by a considerable number of modern publishing and printing houses.

Very often, as the visitor will see, the printer's mark is, in its way, a really beautiful piece of design; many have an interest as being associated with the reputation of a famous printer like Caxton, or Aldus, or Elzevier; while others depend mainly for their point upon some special symbolic meaning, very frequently taking the form of an illustrated pun. Thus, in the West Corridor, the mark of Lotter—which means "vagrant" in German—is a mendicant supplicating alms. In the South Corridor, the mark of Geoffroy Tory commemorates the death of his little daughter—the broken vase, with a book symbolizing the literary studies of which she had been fond.

There is no necessity, however, of describing the marks in detail, for, with the exception of two or three American examples, they were all taken from William Roberts's *Printers' Marks* (London, 1893), in which they are illustrated and explained. Those thought best adapted for decorative effect were chosen throughout, although the marks of as many of the better-known printers as possible were

The Printers' Marks

included. Occasionally a border or a motto was omitted, but in the main Roberts's engravings were copied. In the West Corridor the marks are mostly those of German printers; in the South Corridor, French; in the East Corridor, Italian and Spanish; in the North Corridor, English and Scottish and American.[1]

Roland Hinton Perry's
Bas-Reliefs

Perry's bas-reliefs, at the west end of the North and South Corridors, have already been referred to. They are four in number in the vaults and measure 3 feet 8 inches from one side to another. Taken as a series they represent what may be called, for lack of a better title, *Ancient Prophetic Inspiration*. The chief figure in each is a sibyl or priestess—Greek, Roman, Persian, Scandinavian—in the act of delivering the prophetic warnings which have been revealed to her in the rapture of a divine frenzy. She is regarded as the mouthpiece of the god and, therefore, as the fountain of religion, wisdom, literature, art, and success in war—all of

[1]The following is the list, beginning, in each corridor, at the lefthand end of the outer wall. The dates appended to the names are from William Roberts's book: West Corridor—Wolfgang Koepfel 1523; Johann Fust and Peter Schoeffer, 1457; Craft Mueller, 1536–1562; Conrad Baumgarten, 1503–1505; Jacobus Pfortzheim, 1488–1518; Cratander, 1519; Valentin Kobian, 1532–1542; Martin Schott, 1498; Melchior Lotter, 1491–1536; Theodosius and Josias Rihel, 1535–1639. South Corridor—Rutger Velpius (Flemish), 1553–1614; François Estienne, 1525; Simon de Colines, 1520; François Regnault, early part of the sixteenth century; Simon Vostre, 1488–1528; Sebastien Nivelle, latter part of the sixteenth century; Martin Morin, 1484–1518; Sebastien Gryphius, second quarter of the sixteenth century; André Wéchel, 1535; Geoffroy Tory, 1524; Guillaume Chandière, 1564; Pierre Le Rouge, 1488; Mathurin Breuille, 1562–1583 Etienne Dolet, 1540; Jehan Treschel, 1493; Jehan Petit, 1525. East Corridor—Paul and Anthony Meietos (Italian), 1570; Gian Giacomo di Legrano (Italian), 1503–1533; Juan Rosenbach (Spanish), 1493–1526; Andrea Torresano (Italian), 1481–1540; Valentin Fernandez (Spanish), 1501; Christopher Plantin (Flemish), 1557; Daniel Elzevier (Dutch, the mark of the Sage), 1617–1625; the Brothers Sabio (Italian), early part of the sixteenth century; Melchior Sessa (Italian), sixteenth century; Ottaviano Scotto (Italian), 1480–1520; Giammaria Rizzardi (Italian), latter part of the eighteenth century; Filippo Giunta (Italian), 1515; Lucantonio Giunta (Italian), 1500; Aldus Manutius (Italian), 1502. North Corridor—D. Appleton & Co.; the DeVinne Press; Charles Scribner's Sons; Harper & Brothers; Houghton Mifflin & Co. (the Riverside Press); the Century Co.; J. B. Lippincott Co.; Dodd, Mead & Co.; William Caxton, 1489; Richard Grafton, 1537–1572; Thomas Vautrollier (Edinburgh and London), 1556–1605; John Day, 1546–1584; William Jaggard, 1595–1624; Alexander Arbuthnot (Edinburgh), 1580; Andrew Hester, 1550; Richard Pynson, 1493–1527. Of the marks in this last corridor, those on the north are of American houses, all contemporary, and on the south, of early English and Scottish printers and publishers.

116

which are typified, in one panel or another, in the figures of her auditors.

Beginning in the South Corridor, the first panel shows the Cumaean or Roman Sibyl. She is represented, in accordance with the ancient histories, as an old and withered hag, whose inspiration comes from an infernal, rather than a celestial source. Two figures, as in all the panels, complete Perry's group, one male and the other female. The first is clad in the splendid armor of a Roman general; the woman is nude and stands for Roman Art and Literature. At her feet is a box of manuscripts, and she takes in one hand an end of the long scroll (representing one of the Sibylline Brooks, so famous in Roman history) which the priestess holds in her lap. The panel on the other side of the arch represents a Scandinavian Vala or Wise Woman, with streaming hair and a wolfskin over her head and shoulders. She typifies, in her bold gesture and excited gaze, the barbaric inspiration of the northern nations. To the left is the figure of a Norse warrior, and to the right a naked woman lies stretched upon the ground, personifying the vigorous life and fecundity of genius of the North.

In the North Corridor, the subjects of Perry's two decorations are Greek and Persian Inspiration. The former is represented by the priestess of the world-renowned Oracle of Apollo at Delphi. She is seated upon a tripod, placed above a mysterious opening in the earth, from which the sacred fumes rise to intoxicate the priestess, and fill her with the spirit of prophecy. On one side of the panel, an old man, standing for Greek science and philosophy, takes down her words on a tablet; on the other is a nude female figure, personifying Greek art and literature. In the second panel, that of Persia, the face of the Sibyl is veiled, to signify the occult wisdom of the East. A man prostrates himself at her feet in a fervor of religious devotion, and a woman, nearly nude, stands listening in the background. With her voluptuous figure and her ornaments of pearl and gold—a fillet, anklets, armlets, and necklace—she represents the luxuriance and sensuousness of Eastern art and poetry.

THE WEST CORRIDOR

Walter Shirlaw's Paintings The subjects of Shirlaw's figures in the vault of the West Corridor are, on the west, beginning at the left: Zoology, Physics, Mathematics, and Geology; and on the east, again beginning at the left: Archaeology, Botany, Astronomy, and Chemistry. Each science is represented by a female figure about 7½ feet in height. The figures are especially interesting, aside from their artistic merit, for the variety of symbolism by which every science is distinguished from the others, and for the subtlety with which much of this symbolism is expressed. Not only is each accompanied by various appropriate objects, but the lines of the drapery, the expression of the face and body, and the color itself are, wherever practicable, made to subserve the idea of the science represented. Thus the predominant colors used in the figure of Chemistry—purple, blue, and red—are the ones which occur most often in chemical experimenting. In the pendentive of Geology, Shirlaw employs principally purple and orange; the former is the ruling color in many of the more common rock formations when seen in the mass and naturally; and the latter is the color of the ordinary lichens one finds on boulders and ledges. In the matter of line, again, the visitor will notice a very marked difference between the abrupt, broken line used in the drapery of Archaeology and the moving, flowing line in that of Physics. In both cases it will be found that the line is in very complete sympathy with the character of the science depicted. The method of archaeology is largely excavation carried on among sculptural and architectural fragments. The swirling drapery of Physics is suggestive of flame and heat.

Zoology is represented with a lion seated beside her, her hands clasping his mane. She is the huntress and student of wild life, and her body is powerfully developed, like an Amazon's. She is clad in the pelt of an animal, the head forming her cap, and in buskins of skin. She stands on a rocky piece of ground, like a desert. The chief colors employed in the pendentive are the typical animal colors, browns and yellows.

Physics stands on an electric globe, from which emanate rays of light. She carries a torch in her left hand, and she holds up an end of her drapery in her right in such a way

Photo: Anne Day

Mathematics holding a scroll with geometric figures. One of eight panels by Walter Shirlaw in the West Corridor of the second floor.

that it seems to start from the flame and flow in sympathy with it over her whole body, so that it conveys the idea of the unceasing motion of fire. The same colors as those used in the pendentive of Geology, purple and orange, are used here also, but in this case standing, of course, for the colors of flame.

Mathematics, the exact science, is represented as almost entirely nude, like "the Naked Truth" of Walker's lunette on the floor below. Her right foot is on a stone block inscribed with the conic sections, and on a scroll which she holds are various geometrical figures. Her scanty drapery is appropriately disposed in the severest lines.

Geology, a sculpturesque figure, stands squarely and firmly upon a mountain top, beyond which is seen the setting sun. A fold of her drapery forms a receptacle for the specimens she has gathered. In her left hand is a globe, and in her right a fossil shell. Her hair is confined by a headdress of bars of silver and gold. The embroidered pattern of her garment has a suggestion of fossil forms and of the little lizards which are found among the rocks.

Archaeology is clad in the Roman costume, and wears the helmet of Minerva; the helmet is wreathed with olive, the emblem of peace, which was sacred to Minerva, and is here used with special reference to the peaceful character of the science, which can pursue its labors only in an orderly society. The figure stands on a block of stone, the surface of which is carved to represent a scroll, the ancient form of book. A vase, copied from the manufacture of the Zuñi Indians of New Mexico stands beside her. In her right hand she holds a large book, the pages of which she examines with the aid of a magnifying glass in order to spell out its half-obliterated text. Around her neck is coiled a chameleon, whose changing hues are intended to symbolize the varying nature of the theories she propounds.

The countenance of Botany is expressive of a joyous sympathy with nature. She stands on the pad of a water lily, engaged in analyzing its flower, the long stem of which coils gracefully about her body to the water. Her drapery flows and breaks as a half-opened flower might arrange itself.

Astronomy holds a lens, such as is used in a telescope, in her right hand, and in her left the globe of Saturn surrounded by its rings—selected as being perhaps the best

Photo: Anne Day

Geology with a fossil in one hand and a globe in the other. One of the panels by Walter Shirlaw in the West Corridor of the second floor.

119

known and most easily distinguished of all the planets. She stands on the sphere of the earth, beyond which, to the left, is the quarter moon. The lines of her drapery with their slow curves are suggestive, in a way, of the orbits of the heavenly bodies. They flow in long lines, enveloping her figure in the strength which proceeds from complete harmony.

Chemistry is shown with her left foot placed upon a piece of chemical apparatus and holding in her right hand a glass retort, in which she is distilling a liquid. The necessary heat, manifested by the ascending vapor which curls about the vessel, is from the mouth of the serpent—the emblem of fecundity and life, breathing the element of life, fire. The serpent is coiled about an hourglass, which is significant of the exact measurement of time necessary in chemical experiments. The face of the figure is more worn, on account of the anxious nature of her employment, than would comport with the character of an out-of-door science like Botany or Zoology. She is draped somewhat in the Eastern manner, like a sibyl, thus recalling the occult character ascribed to the science during the Middle Ages—when it was called alchemy—and, for that matter, the marvelousness of its results in the laboratories of today. A snake wound as a fillet about her hair still further emphasizes this mystic quality.

At either end of the corridor is a tablet bearing a list of names of men distinguished in the sciences which Shirlaw has depicted; at the north end: Cuvier, the Zoologist; Linnaeus, the Botanist; Schliemann, the Archaeologist; and Copernicus, the Astronomer; at the south end: Lagrange, the Mathematician; Lavoisier, the Chemist; Rumford, the Physicist; and Lyell, the Geologist. In the penetrations on either side of these two lists of names are the following appropriate inscriptions:

> The first creature of God was the light of sense; the last was the light of reason.   —Bacon

> The Light shineth in darkness, and the darkness comprehendeth not.   —John 1:5

> All are but parts of one stupendous whole, Whose body Nature is, and God the soul.
>   —Pope

> In nature all is useful, all is beautiful.
>   —Emerson

Along the center of the vault, three medallions by William B. Van Ingen represent respectively Sculpture, Architecture, and Painting. In each the art is represented by a female figure engaged either in chiseling the features of a bust (that of Washington), drawing the plan of a building, or painting at an easel.

In walking along the West Corridor the visitor will notice, in the middle of the west wall, what was the original Declaration of Independence Shrine. The famous document was displayed here from 1924 to 1952 before being moved to the Archives Building on Constitution Avenue. Designed by Francis Bacon, brother of Henry Bacon, the architect of the Lincoln Memorial, it consists of a wall case beneath a curved pediment within which is the Great Seal of the United States. Two bronze eagles are set against the wall to either side of the frame. Beneath the frame is a gray marble display case resting on massive voluted supports ending in lion's paws.

Former Shrine of the Declaration of Independence

THE NORTH CORRIDOR

Passing to the North Corridor, the attention is at once attracted to the brilliant coloring of Reid's decorations in the vault and along the north wall. The former are five in number, and represent the Five Senses. They are octagonal in form, measuring within an inch of 6½ feet across. The order of the subjects, beginning at the westerly end, is Taste, Sight, Smell, Hearing, Touch. In each the sense suggested is represented by a beautiful young woman, more of the modern than the antique type of beauty, and clad in drapery which recalls contemporary fashions rather than the classic conventions which are usually followed by artists in their treatment of ideal subjects. Being painted upon a ceiling, so that the visitor is required to look directly upward in order to study them, the figures, though, in a sense, represented as seated, are rather to be imagined as poised in the air, without any special reference to the law of gravitation. They are shown as supported upon cloud banks, and the backgrounds of the panels are sky and clouds.

Robert Reid's Paintings

Touch with a butterfly on her arm and a setter at back. One of the Five Senses by Robert Reid in the North Corridor of the second floor.

Hearing with a shell at her ear. One of the Five Senses by Robert Reid in the North Corridor of the second floor.

The suggestion of the subject is as simply as it is ingeniously and unconventionally conveyed. A large portion of this suggestion must be looked for, of course, in the expression of the faces and the attitudes as well as in the action of the figures. Taste is shown drinking from a shell. She is surrounded by foliage, and a vine grows beside her laden with bunches of ripe grapes. She wears flowers in her hair, and the idea throughout may perhaps be taken as that of the autumnal feast of the wine press. Sight is looking at her reflection in a handglass, and smiling with pleasure at the evidence of her beauty. A splendid peacock, the emblem of beauty and pride in beauty, is introduced beside her. Smell is represented seated beside a bank of lilies and roses. From this mass of flowers she has selected a great white rose, which she presses to her nose. Hearing holds a large sea shell to her ear, and dreamily listens to its roaring. Touch is delightedly observing a butterfly which has alighted on her bare outstretched arm—the touch of its tiny feet as it walks over her flesh imparting an unaccustomed sensation to her nerves. A setter dog, which she has just ceased from caressing, lies asleep behind her.

Reid's subjects in the four circular panels along the wall are entitled, in order from left to right: *Wisdom, Understanding, Knowledge,* and *Philosophy.* Each is represented by a half-length seated female figure—more solidly painted, but of much the same type as the figures representing the Senses—holding a scroll, book, or tablet. In the panel of Philosophy, a Greek temple is seen in the background, emblematic of the Greek origin of philosophy.

Alternating with Reid's ceiling paintings is a series of rectangular panels, in which are depicted, in low tones of color and in a style somewhat suggestive of a classic bas-relief, a number of ancient outdoor athletic contests. Beginning at the west end of the vault, the first of these represents a group of young men throwing the discus. Then come Wrestling and Running. In the fourth panel, the athletes are being rubbed down by attendants, to clear them of the sweat and heat of the conflict; and in the fifth, the successful contestants are kneeling to receive the crown of victory at the hands of a woman seated on a dais. The last picture represents the return home, a tripping company of youths and maidens crowned with garlands.

The visitor will remember what was said concerning the special enrichment of the penetrations in the side corridors for the sake of compensating in a way for the absence of such decorations as Shirlaw's in the pendentives. In the present instance, this enrichment takes the form of griffons and swans, which serve as "supporters" of the panels containing the printers' marks.

In the pendentives, tablets for inscriptions alternate with medallions containing trophies of various trades and sciences. The list of the latter, beginning at the left over the north wall, is as follows: Geometry, represented by a compass, a protractor, and a scroll, cone, and cylinder; Meteorology, the barometer, thermometer, and anemometer; Forestry, a growing tree, and an axe and pruning knife; Navigation, the chronometer, log, rope, rudder, and compass; Mechanics, the lever, wedge, and pulley block; and Transportation, with a piston, propeller, driving wheel, and locomotive headlight.

The inscriptions are from Adelaide A. Procter's poem "Unexpressed," and are as follows:

> Dwells within the soul of every Artist
> More than all his effort can express
>
> No great Thinker ever lived and taught you
> All the wonder that his soul received.
>
> No true painter set on canvas
> All the glorious vision he conceived.
>
> No musician. . . .
> But be sure he heard, and strove to render,
> Feeble echoes of celestial strains.
>
> Love and Art united
> Are twin mysteries, different yet the same.
>
> Love may strive, but vain is the endeavor
> All its boundless riches to unfold.
>
> Art and Love speak; and their words must be
> Like sighings of illimitable forests.

The only other decoration which there is space to mention is the broad, semicircular border which follows the line of the vault on the wall at either end of the corridor. At the east end, this border is ornamented with a bright-colored arabesque, mainly in violet and greens, with a medallion in the center bearing a map of the Western Hemisphere. At the west end, the border is plainer, with five semicircular or circular tablets, two of which are ornamented with the obverse and reverse respectively of the Great Seal of the United States. The other three carry the following inscriptions:

> Order is Heaven's first law.   —Pope
>
> Memory is the treasurer and guardian of all things.
>   —Cicero
>
> Beauty is the creator of the universe.   —Emerson

THE EAST CORRIDOR

George Randolph Barse,
Jr.'s Paintings

In the East Corridor, the pendentive figures of Barse represent, beginning on the east side, at the north end Lyric Poetry (entitled by the artist *Lyrica*), Tragedy, Comedy, and History; and on the west, again beginning at the north, Love Poetry (Erotica), Tradition, Fancy, and Romance.

The subject of the entire series, therefore, may be called simply Literature. The figures, as the visitor will perceive, need but little explanation. All are those of women clad in graceful, classic robes, represented throughout as seated, and depicted with little attempt at dramatic expression or action. Lyric Poetry is playing on the lyre. Tragedy and Comedy have a tragic and comic mask respectively, and Comedy a tambourine. History has a scroll and palm branch, and an ancient book box for scrolls, such as was used by the Romans, is set at her feet. Romance has a pen and a scroll (see Plate XVI between pages 16 and 17). Fancy clasps her hands, and gazes upward with a rapt expression on her face. Tradition wears the aegis, and holds a statue of the winged goddess of Victory in her hand—both introduced as symbols of antiquity. Erotica is writing on a tablet.

Photo: The Library of Congress

Lyrica, Lyric Poetry, with a lyre, by George Randolph Barse, Jr. One of eight panels in the East Corridor of the second floor.

Photo: The Library of Congress

Tragedy with a tragic mask in her right hand, by George Randolph Barse, Jr. One of eight panels in the East Corridor of the second floor.

Comedy with a comic mask by
George Randolph Barse, Jr. One of
eight panels in the East Corridor of
the second floor.

History with a scroll and a palm
branch, by George Randolph Barse,
Jr. One of eight panels in the East
Corridor of the second floor.

William Andrew Mackay's Paintings

Along the center of the vault, occupying a similar position to the medallions in the opposite corridor, is another series of three paintings, executed by William Andrew Mackay, which represent the Life of Man. One will best understand the meaning of the paintings by first reading the inscriptions which are placed immediately above and below each medallion. On one side they refer to the ancient allegory of the Three Fates, Clotho, Lachesis, and Atropos—the first of whom spun, the second wove, and the third cut the Thread of Life—and are as follows:

> For a web begun God sends thread.
> —Old Proverb

> The web of life . . . is of a mingled yarn, good and ill together.
> —Shakespeare, *All's Well that Ends Well*

> Comes the blind Fury with th' abhorred shears
> And slits the thin-spun life.   —Milton

126

On the other side the inscriptions, which compare the life of a man to the life of a tree, are taken from Cardinal Wolsey's speech in *Henry VIII:*

> This is the state of man: to-day he puts forth
> The tender leaves of hopes.
>
>   To-morrow blossoms,
> And bears his blushing honors thick upon him.
>
> The third day comes a frost, . . .
> And . . . nips his root,
> And then he falls.

Accordingly, in the present series, the first medallion shows Clotho with her distaff and a baby lying in her lap. The sun is rising above the horizon, a sapling begins to put out its branches, and near by is a little spring. In the next picture, Lachesis has a loom and shuttle. The spring has grown into a river, and the mature man bears in his hand a basket of fruit gathered from the abundance of the full-grown tree, while the sun in the heavens marks the high noon of life. In the last medallion the sun is setting, the tree has fallen in ruin on the ground, and the stream has dried up. The man, grown old and crippled, faints by the roadside, and Atropos opens her fatal shears to sever the thread of his existence.

At each end of the corridor is a tablet containing the names of eminent American printers, and men who have contributed to the improvement of American printing machinery. At the north these names are: Green, Daye, Franklin, Thomas, Bradford; and at the south, Clymer, Adams, Gordon, Hoe, Bruce.

THE SOUTH CORRIDOR

Benson's decorations in the vault of the South Corridor and along the wall below are of the same size and shape as those of Robert Reid in the North Corridor. The arabesque ornament of the ceiling is so arranged, however, as to allow space for only three instead of five of these hexagonal panels. The subject of the paintings they contain is the Graces—Aglaia (at the east (see Plate XVII between pages 16 and 17)), Thalia (in the center) and Euphrosyne (at the west).

Frank Weston Benson's Paintings

127

Aglaia, patroness of husbandry, with a shepherd's crook. One of the Three Graces by Frank Weston Benson in the vault of the South Corridor of the second floor.

The three figures are almost invariably represented in a group, in both ancient and modern art. Taken together, they stand, of course, for beauty and graciousness, and typify, also, the agreeable arts and occupations. In separating them, Benson has considered Aglaia as the patroness of Husbandry; Thalia as representing Music; and Euphrosyne, Beauty. The first, therefore, has a shepherd's crook, the second a lyre, and the last is looking at her reflection in a hand mirror. All are shown sitting in the midst of a pleasant summer landscape, with trees and water and fertile meadows.

For the four circular panels Benson has chosen as his subject the Seasons. Each is represented by a beautiful half-length figure of a young woman, with no attempt, however, at any elaborate symbolism to distinguish the season which she typifies. Such distinction as the painter has chosen to indicate is to be sought rather in the character of the faces, or in the warmer or colder coloring of the whole panel—in a word, in the general artistic treatment.

At either end of the vault is a rectangular panel painted in the same style as those depicting the ancient games in the North Corridor, but in this case representing the modern sports of Football and Baseball. The former, occurring at the east end of the vault, is a more or less realistic picture of a "scrimmage." The latter is more conventionalized, showing single figures, like the pitcher and catcher, in the attitude of play, and others with bats, masks, and gloves.

Instead of the swans and dragons of the North Corridor, the printers' marks in the penetrations of the present corridor are supported between the figures of mermen and fauns, and mermaids and nymphs, the male figures, with their suggestion of greater decorative strength, occuring at the ends of the corridor, and the nymphs and mermaids alternating between. Altogether there are thirty-two figures, each painted by Frederick C. Martin.

On the pendentives, the series of trophies begun in the North Corridor is continued, giving place, as before, in every other pendentive, to a tablet bearing an inscription. Beginning on the south side, at the east end, the trophies are as follows: Printing, with a stick, ink ball, and type case; Pottery, three jugs of different kinds of clay; Glass-

Photo: The Library of Congress

Spring, one of the Four Seasons, painted in the round on the wall of the South Corridor of the second floor. Frank Weston Benson, painter.

IT IS THE MIND THAT MAKES THE MAN
AND OVR VIGOR
IS IN OVR IMMORTAL SOVL.

129

making, three glass vases of different shapes; Carpentry, a saw, bit, hammer, and right angle; Smithery, the anvil, pincers, hammer, bolt, and nut; Masonry, a trowel, square, plumb, and mortarboard.

The following are the eight inscriptions:

> Studies perfect nature and are perfected by experience.
> —Bacon

> Dreams, books, are each a world; and books, we know,
> Are a substantial world, both pure and good.
> —Wordsworth

> Learning is but an adjunct to ourself,
> —Shakespeare, *Love's Labor's Lost*

> A little learning is a dangerous thing;
> Drink deep, or taste not the Pierian spring.   —Pope

> The universal cause
> Acts to one end, but acts by various laws.   —Pope

> Vain, very vain, [the] weary search to find
> That bliss which only centres in the mind.
> —Goldsmith

> Creation's heir, the world, the world is mine!
> —Goldsmith

> The fault . . . is not in our stars,
> But in ourselves, that we are underlings.
> —Shakespeare, *Julius Caesar*

The semicircular borders at either end are practically the same in color and design as in the North Corridor. At the east end, the Eastern is substituted for the Western Hemisphere, and at the west end, a caduceus and a lictor's axe for the United States Seal. The accompanying inscriptions are as follows:

> Man raises but time weighs.
> —Modern Greek proverb

> Beneath the rule of men entirely great,
> The pen is mightier than the sword.
> —Bulwer Lytton

> The noblest motive is the public good.
> —Virgil

THE DECORATION OF THE CORRIDOR WALLS

The decoration of the vaults of the four corridors is distinctly Renaissance in character; the walls beneath, however, are colored and decorated in accordance with a Pompeiian motive. It may seem at first thought illogical thus to join two styles so remote from each other in point of time, but it must be remembered that, in both art and literature, the Renaissance was literally, as has been pointed out, the *new birth* of Greek and Roman forms, in the course of which the Italian painters adapted to their use and subdued to their style the sort of wall decoration which we know as Pompeiian, from the discovery of so many examples of it in the excavations at Pompeii. The two styles, as used in conjunction in the Library of Congress, not only in these corridors but throughout the building, are perfectly harmonious in color and design; from the explanation just given the visitor will see that they have long ago been brought into a historical unity as well, through the conventions established by the great and authoritative school of the Renaissance artists.

The frequent occurrence of windows, doors, and pilasters cuts the wall into narrow spaces, which at the north and south, are colored a plain olive, and at the east and west the familiar rich Pompeiian red, ornamented with simple arabesques and, at the ends, with female figures representing the Virtues, by George Willoughby Maynard. There are eight of these figures in all, two in each corner of the hall. Each figure is about 5½ feet high, clad in floating classic drapery, and represented to the spectator as appearing before him in the air, without a support or background other than the deep red of the wall. The style of the paintings is Pompeiian; the general tone is somewhat like that of marble, although touched with color so as to remove any comparison with the marble framing.

George Willoughby Maynard's Pompeiian Panels

Beginning at the left in each case, the names and order of the Virtues are as follows: At the northeast corner, Fortitude and Justice; at the southeast corner, Patriotism and Courage; at the southwest corner, Temperance and Prudence; at the northwest corner, Industry and Concord. The number of virtues to be represented was determined beforehand, of course, by the number of spaces at the disposal of the painter. The selection, therefore, was necessarily somewhat arbitrary.

Each figure is shown with certain characteristic attributes. In the case of Industry, Courage, and Patriotism,

Justice, with a globe in one hand and a sword in the other, by George Willoughby Maynard. In the northeast corner next to the East Corridor of the second floor.

Maynard has himself selected these attributes; in the other five figures he has followed the usual conventions.

Fortitude is shown fully armed—the mace in her right hand and the buckler on her arm, and protected by cuirass, casque, and greaves. She is thus represented as ready for any emergency—living in continual expectation of danger, and constantly prepared to meet it. Justice holds the globe in her right hand, signifying the extent of her sway. She holds a naked sword upright, signifying the terribleness of her punishment. Patriotism is feeding an eagle, the emblem of America, from a golden bowl—an action which symbolizes the high nourishment with which the Virtue sustains the spirit of the country. Courage is represented as armed hastily with the buckler, casque, and sword—not, like Fortitude, continually on guard, but snatching up her arms in the presence of an unforeseen danger. Temperance—figured as the classic rather than the modern virtue—holds an antique pitcher in her right hand, from which a stream of some liquid, whether wine or water, descends into the bowl she holds in her left. Her buoyancy and air of health betoken her moderation of living. Prudence looks in a hand glass to discover any danger which may assail her from behind. In her right hand she holds a serpent— the emblem of wisdom. Industry draws the flax from a distaff, the end of which is stuck in her girdle, and twists it into thread, to be wound upon the spindle which hangs at her side. Concord—the Roman goddess Concordia— illustrates the blessings of peace. In her right hand she bears an olive branch, and in her left she carries a cornucopia filled with wheat.

The Inscriptions along the Walls

Before taking leave of the corridors, one more feature of the decoration requires notice—namely, the twenty-nine inscriptions occupying the gilt tablets below the stucco frames which surround the circular windows and the wall paintings of Benson and Reid. They are as follows:

Too low they build who build beneath the stars.   —Young

There is but one temple in the Universe and that
    is the Body of Man.   —Novalis

Beholding the bright countenance of Truth in the
    quiet and still air of delightful studies.   —Milton

The true university of these days is a collection of books.
          —Carlyle

Nature is the art of God.   —Sir Thomas Browne

There is no work of genius which has not been
    the delight of mankind.   —Lowell

It is the mind that makes the man, and our vigor
    is in our immortal soul.   —Ovid

They are never alone that are accompanied by
    noble thoughts.   —Sidney

Man is one world and has
    Another to attend him.   —Herbert

Tongues in trees, books in the running brooks,
    Sermons in stones, and good in everything.
         —Shakespeare, *As You Like It*

The true Shekinah is man.   —Chrysostom

Only the actions of the just
    Smell sweet and blossom in the dust.   —Shirley

Art is long, and Time is fleeting.   —Longfellow

The history of the world is the biography
    of great men.   —Carlyle

Books will speak plain when counsellors blanch.   —Bacon

Glory is acquired by virtue but preserved by letters. —Petrarch

The foundation of every state is the education of its youth.
         —Dionysius

The chief glory of every people arises from its authors.
         —Dr. Johnson

There is only one good, namely knowledge, and
    one only evil, namely ignorance.   —Diogenes Laertius

Knowledge comes, but wisdom lingers.   —Tennyson

Wisdom is the principal thing; therefore get wisdom:
    and with all thy getting get understanding. —Proverbs 4:7

Ignorance is the curse of God,
    Knowledge the wing wherewith we fly to heaven.
         —2 Henry IV

How charming is divine Philosophy!   —Milton

Books must follow sciences and not sciences books.   —Bacon

In books lies the Soul of the whole past time.   —Carlyle

Words are also actions and actions are a kind of words.
         —Emerson

Reading maketh a full man, conference a ready man,
    and writing an exact man.   —Bacon

Science is organized knowledge.   —Herbert Spencer

Beauty is truth, truth beauty.   —Keats

THE GALLERIES AND PAVILIONS

Gold wings set in a square coffer with egg-and-dart molding. Ceiling decoration of the South Gallery of the second floor.

Having explored the corridors the visitor turns to the galleries and pavilions of the second floor. The rooms on the second floor were intended for the most part as exhibition halls for the display of works of art which have come into the possession of the Library through the operation of the copyright law, or of books and manuscripts of special interest on account of their rarity and curiosity.

There is space here to speak only of the more richly decorated of these rooms—the corner pavilions and the two galleries on the west side. The others, as the visitor will see in walking through them, require no special description. The walls are decorated in broad masses of plain color, with deep friezes of simple but interesting patterns. The decoration varies from room to room, but all are united in a single intelligent harmony of color. Each contains a long skylight surrounded by a stucco border left plain in most of the galleries, but in the South Gallery enriched by coffering decorated with gilt "cherubs' wings." The skylights are ornamented with a simple design of stained glass. The chief colors employed are purple and pale green and yellow, and the design includes the names of men distinguished in art, letters, and science.[1]

[1]In the South Gallery, the names are those of the signers of the Declaration of Independence. In the Southeast Gallery, those of inventors: Gutenberg, Daguerre, Schwartz, Montgolfier, Watt, Cooper, Stevens, Newcomen, Trevithick, Hargreaves, Corliss, Arkwright, Jacquard, Fitch, Fuller, Wood, Wheatstone, Whitney, Morse, Vail, Goodyear, Ericsson, Hoe, McCormick, Howe, Bessemer, Westinghouse, Edison, and Bell.

Architects and engineers are commemorated in the Northeast Gallery; Ictinus, Vitruvius, Anthemius, Palladio, Vignola, Sansovino, Bramante, Brunelleschi, Michelangelo, Lescot, Duc, Delorme, Labrouste, Mansard, Bulfinch, Wren, Jones, Walter, Richardson, Hunt, Archimedes, Stephenson, Smeaton, Vauban, Lavally, Jarvis, Eads, Schwedler, Roebling, and Barnard.

In the North Gallery the list is miscellaneous, including theologians, physicians, jurists, scientists, musicians, sculptors, and painters: Lycurgus, Coke, Justinian, Blackstone, Montesquieu, Marshall, Story, Hippocrates, Avicenna, Harvey, Paracelsus, Jenner, Hahnemann, Saint Augustine, Bowditch, Chrysostom, Saint Bernard, Bossuet, Pascal, Edwards, Channing, Euclid, Pythagoras, Pliny, Copernicus, Darwin, Humboldt, Agassiz, Faraday, Mendelssohn, Mozart, Haydn, Bach, Liszt, Wagner, Phidias, Apelles, da Vinci, Giotto, Perugino, Raphael, Titian, Guido Reni, Correggio, Dürer, Palissy, Thorwaldsen, Rembrandt, Rubens, Van Dyck, Murillo, Holbein.

The chief decorations of the gallery into which one goes from the South Corridor of the second floor are two large lunettes by Kenyon Cox, one at each end of the room over the triple doors by which one enters or leaves. For the rest, the room is lighted, like the other galleries, on both sides, so that one may look out toward the Capitol, or, on the east, into one of the interior courts. The ceiling is an elliptical barrel vault, rising to a height of 29 feet. It is set with square coffers in blue and gold, and divided by double ribs which spring from the paired pilasters. Between the pilasters a bright-colored arabesque is introduced, in which blue is the prevailing color. It is continued in the ceiling by an arabesque in relief, the most conspicuous features of which are seated cherubs, and medallions with the letters "C. L."—standing for "Congressional Library." The floor is Vermont, Italian, and Georgia marble, laid in square panels, so as to reflect, in a way, the pattern of the coffers in the ceiling above.

Kenyon Cox's lunettes are 34 feet long and 9½ feet high. *Kenyon Cox's Paintings* At the south end of the room the subject of the decoration is the Sciences, and at the north end, the Arts. The panels are similar in composition, occupying as they do exactly corresponding positions. On each the design is drawn together by a low marble balustrade, at the center of which is a semicircular recess enclosing a kind of throne or high marble seat. At either end of the recess, so as to come directly over a pilaster occurring between the doors, is a post bearing a tripod on which incense is burning. The effect is to carry the lines of the architecture below up into the painting.

In the panel of the Arts, the central throne is occupied by the figure of Poetry, represented as a young and beautiful woman crowned with laurel and bearing an antique lyre. She is seated in an attitude of immediate inspiration, the fold of her garment blowing in the wind, her left hand raised from the chord which she has just struck upon the lyre, and her lips parted in a burst of song. On the steps of her throne are two little winged cherubs, one writing down her words on a tablet, and the other raising his arms in sympathy as he joins in the rhythmical swing of her song.

The Arts *by Kenyon Cox at the north end of the Southwest Gallery on the second floor. At the center is the figure of Poetry with a lyre.*

The first may be taken as personifying the more strictly literary and reflective side of poetry, and the other as standing for its feeling for harmony and music, or, in general, the lyrical element in poetry. In the lefthand portion of the decoration are Architecture and Music, and to the right, Sculpture and Painting—all typified by female figures bearing some appropriate object identifying the art which they represent. Architecture is conceived as the sternest and most dignified of the arts, as shown by her expression of proud abstraction and the severe lines of her drapery. She holds a miniature marble column, and her head is crowned with a circlet of battlements. Music is playing upon a violin, and looking the while upon the pages of a great music book which a kneeling cherub holds open before her. Beside her is a violoncello. Sculpture holds a statuette of a nude female figure, and talks with Painting, who has a palette and brushes. The latter, as representing the gentler and more luxurious art, is shown partly nude, and leaning her head affectionately upon the shoulder of her companion. In the corner of the picture are a vase and two large plates in different styles of decorated pottery— standing for the minor decorative arts.

In the lunette of the Sciences the central figure is Astron-

136

omy. She holds a pair of compasses, and leans forward on her throne to make measurements upon the celestial globe which a cherub holds up before her. Another cherub to the right looks through a telescope. To the left of the panel are Physics and Mathematics. Physics holds an instrument designed to show the law of the balance of different weights at different distances from the point of support. Mathematics has an abacus, or counting frame, with which she is instructing a little cherub in the elements of figures. The beads of the abacus are so placed that they give the date "1896"—the year the picture was painted. Beside her, in the extreme lefthand corner, are various figures illustrating plane and solid geometry. The former kind are so arranged, as the visitor will see by looking carefully, that they form all the letters of the artist's name—KENYON COX. On the other side of the throne are Botany, bearing a young oak tree, and wearing a green and white figured gown, and Zoology, a nude figure holding out her hand to caress a magnificent peacock perched on the coping of the balustrade. In the corner are a shell and various kinds of minerals, for Conchology, Mineralogy, Geology, and so forth.

On tablets over the doors and windows are the names of men distinguished in science and art. Those representing art are Wagner, Mozart, Homer, Milton, Raphael, Rubens, Vitruvius, Mansard, Phidias, and Michelangelo. The scientists are Leibnitz, Galileo, Aristotle, Ptolemy, Dalton, Hipparchus, Herschel, Kepler, Lamarck, and Helmholtz.

THE PAVILION OF THE DISCOVERERS

The Southwest Pavilion—or the Pavilion of the Discoverers, as it may better be called, from the subject of the paintings with which it is ornamented—opens immediately from the Southwest Gallery. The domed ceiling is richly coffered and profusely ornamented with gilding, except for a large central space in the form of a disc, which contains a painted decoration. Below the dome are four lunettes, also occupied by paintings. The walls are ornamented with paired pilasters, bearing a narrow frieze decorated with lions' heads and festoons of garlands.

In the pendentives is a series of four large circular plaques in relief, representing the Seasons. The series, which is repeated in each of the other three pavilions, is the work of Bela Lyon Pratt. Spring, with the label *Seed,* is the figure of a girl sowing the seed, her garment blown into graceful swirls by the early winds of March. Summer is a maturer figure, sitting, quiet and thoughtful, in a field of poppies and is labeled *Bloom.* Autumn is a mother nursing a baby. An older child—a little boy—stands beside her, and the abundance and fruitfulness of the season are still further typified in the ripe bunches of grapes which hang from the vine. It is identified as *Fruit.* Winter, with the sign *Decay,* is an old woman gathering faggots for the hearth. Behind her is a leafless tree, on which is perched an owl. A garland appropriate to the season hangs over each of the four plaques—fruits for Spring and Summer, grains for Autumn, and oak leaves and acorns for Winter.

The paintings in the lunettes and the disc are the work of George Willoughby Maynard, whose panels in the second-floor corridors have already been described. In the lunettes the sequence of Maynard's subjects begins on the east side and continues to the right, as follows: Adventure, Discovery, Conquest, Civilization—the bold roving spirit of Adventure leading to Discovery, which in turn results in Conquest, bringing at last a settled occupation of the land and final Civilization. In the disc of the ceiling, Maynard has depicted the four qualities most appropriate to these four stages of a country's development—Courage, Valor, Fortitude, and Achievement.

Since the lunettes are the same in shape and of the same size, measuring each 31 feet by 6, and since all stand in the same relation toward the whole room, Maynard has followed throughout a single method of arrangement. Each lunette is over three doors or three windows, as the case may be. In accordance, therefore, with this exactly balanced architectural scheme, a pyramidal group of three female figures—pyramidal because any other form would have looked top-heavy—is placed above the central opening. Balancing or, so to say, subsidiary figures, which, if only from their position at the diminishing ends of the lunette, are necessarily of less importance, are placed over the doors or windows to the side. Thus the decoration is poised in complete accordance with the disposition of the wall which it crowns. The figures at the ends, it will be noticed, are of two sorts, mermaids and emblazoned shields; but since they alternate in pairs from lunette to lunette, the shields occurring in the east and west and the mermaids in the north and south, this variety serves very well to accentuate the unity of the composition of the four paintings. The ornament, also, is the same in its more important features: the throne of the center, flanked by cornucopias; the arabesque border with its dolphins, suggestive of seafaring; and the lists of names of discoverers and colonizers which occupy the spaces to the right and left of the central group, and serve to draw together the whole composition.

It would be well if the visitor were to hold in mind these points, for in the two following pavilions on this floor, where the conditions governing the painter are exactly the same as in the present room, it will be seen that the artists employed have followed in their work the same orderly and logical plan of arrangement which Maynard has here adopted.

In the first lunette to the east, Adventure, seated on her throne, holds in her right hand a drawn sword, in instant readiness for the combat; her left hand rests upon an upright caduceus, the emblem of Mercury, the god of the traveler, merchant, and thief, and fit, therefore, to be the patron of the restless adventurers who sailed westward in the sixteenth century, impelled as well by a desire for booty as for legitimate trade. To the right and left are seated female figures, representing respectively Spanish and English adventure—the two countries which furnished America with the largest part of its early buccaneers and adventurers. Like the central figure, the two are clad in rich and elaborate armor, accurately copied, as is that in the other lunettes, from authentic sixteenth-century models. The figure to the left, typifying England, holds a cutlass in her right hand, while her left hand buries itself in a heap of pieces of eight, the pirate and buccaneering coin *par excellence*. The companion figure to the right holds a battleaxe in her right hand, and in her left one of the little figurines, or miniature idols of gold, which the Spaniards in Peru sought so eagerly, and with so much cruelty, to secure from the natives. At either side of the throne is a shield,

139

on which an old Norse Viking ship, propelled by oars and sail, is depicted. At either end of the lunette is a shield, that to the right bearing the arms of Spain, and that to the left those of England. On the Spanish side of the decoration is the following list of names of Spanish adventurers: Díaz, Narvaez, Coello, Cabeza, Verrazano, Bastidas. On the other side is the English list: Drake, Cavendish, Raleigh, Smith, Frobisher, Gilbert. Each group of names is surmounted by the heraldic form of the naval crown, ornamented with alternate sterns and squaresails of ships, which was given by the Romans to a successful naval commander, or to the sailor who first boarded an enemy's ship. In either corner of the lunette still another emblem of sea power, the trident, is introduced.

In the second lunette on the south, Discovery, crowned with a laurel wreath of gold and wearing a leather jerkin, sits on her throne, holding a ship's rudder in her right hand, and with her left upon a globe of the earth, which is supported on her knee. The rude map of America, which appears on it, is copied from a portion of a mappemonde, or chart of the world, which was discovered in England, and which has been ascribed to Leonardo da Vinci. It dates from the second decade of the sixteenth century. The two seated figures to the right and left are clad in armor; the first holds a sword and "Jacob's staff," or cross staff, a device used by the early navigators instead of a quadrant or sextant to determine the altitude of the sun and stars. The figure to the left, with paddle and chart, points toward the distance with outstretched arm, and turns to her companions to beckon them onward. The two shields at the foot of the throne bear an astrolabe, an obsolete instrument used for the same purpose as the cross staff. At either end of the lunette, a mermaid, with a seashell for cap, and with seaweed twined about her body, invites the voyagers with strings of pearls and coral. Lists of names occur at the left and right, surmounted, as before, with the naval crown. The first list is: Solis, Orellana, Van Horn, Oieda, Columbus, Pinzon; the second, Cabot, Magellan, Hudson, Behring, Vespucius (Vespucci), Balboa.

In the third lunette, which is on the west side, that of Conquest, the idea expressed in the central group is that of the proud tranquility which follows triumph in battle. The figures carry the insignia of victory. The one seated upon

Photo: Anne Day

the throne has pushed back her casque and lets her left hand hang idly over the crosspiece of the sword. But there is still danger of a renewal of the struggle; the right hand rests clenched upon an arm of the throne, the armor has not yet been laid aside, and the sword not yet sheathed. The figures to the left and right are in a like attitude of readiness, though they carry an addition to their swords the emblems of peace—the first, representing Southern Conquests, a sheaf of palms; and the second, representing Northern Conquests, chaplets of oak leaves, which wreathe her casque and sword. The two shields bear a heraldic rep-

Ceiling disc in the Southwest Pavilion or Pavilion of the Discoverers on the second floor by George Willoughby Maynard. The figures represent Courage, Value, Fortitude, and Achievement.

141

resentation of the Pillars of Hercules, with the motto *"Ne plus ultra"* twined about them, and between them, in the distance, the setting sun—perhaps an ironic allusion to the ancient idea which set the limits of the earth at the Straits of Gibraltar, or perhaps simply an adaptation and extension of it to the new conditions of knowledge. At the ends of the lunette the arms of England and Spain are again introduced, as significant of the general division of North and South America into English and Spanish territory. The names to the left are: Pizarro, Alvarado, Almagro, Hutten, Frontenac, De Soto; to the right, Cortés, Standish, Winslow, Phipps, Velásquez, De Leon. Over each group is the battlemented mural crown given by the Romans to the soldier who first succeeded in planting a standard upon the wall of a besieged city.

The fourth lunette, Civilization, is the flowering of the other three. The armor has been laid aside, and the three figures in the center are clad simply in classic garments. Civilization, crowned with laurel and seated on her throne, holds up the torch of learning, or enlightenment, and displays the opened page of a book—an idea which is repeated in the lamp and book which compose the device on the two shields below. To the left is Agriculture, crowned with wheat, and holding a scythe and a sheaf of wheat. To the right is Manufactures with distaff and spindle, twisting the thread. The mermaids at the ends of the decoration hold up, one an ear of corn, and the other a branch of the cotton plant bearing both the flower and the boll—the two chief products respectively of the northern and the southern portions of our country. The names are, to the left, Eliot, Calvert, Marquette, Joliet, Oglethorpe, Las Casas; and to the right, Penn, Winthrop, Motolinia, Yeardley, La Salle. Over each list is a wreath of laurel.

Maynard has represented in the ceiling the four qualities most pertinent to the character of his four lunettes. All four are shown as female figures, displayed against a background of arabesque. The first, Courage—a brute, animal courage—is clad in a coat of coarse scale armor, over which a lion's skin is drawn, the head of the beast serving her for a cap. She is armed with a war club and a shield. The next, Valor, is a nobler figure, more beautiful and wearing more beautiful armor. Her right hand holds a sword, and her left is pressed to her breast. The third, Fortitude, is unarmed. In her left arm she carries an architectural column, the emblem of stability. Achievement, the last, is clad in armor but is without offensive weapon. She wears a laurel crown, and in her left hand she carries the Roman standard, surmounted by its eagle and laurel wreath, the symbol of a strong and just government. In the order named, therefore, it will readily be seen how these figures may be said to typify the successive lunettes of Adventure, Discovery, Conquest, and Civilization.

THE PAVILION OF THE ELEMENTS

In the same way that the room decorated by Maynard has been called the Pavilion of the Discoverers, so the Southeast Pavilion may be called the Pavilion of the Elements, from the subject of the paintings ornamenting the lunettes and the disc. The lunettes are by Robert Leftwich Dodge, and the disc by Garnsey and Dodge working in conjunc-

Spring, one of four bas-reliefs in the Southwest Pavilion or Pavilion of the Discoverers on the second floor by Bela Lyon Pratt. The figure is in a round frame with egg-and-dart molding. Above it is a garland of oak leaves and flowers with a quiver of arrows bound by fluttering ribbons.

143

tion, the former making the ornamental design and the latter designing and carrying out the figure work.

Bela Lyon Pratt's Bas-Reliefs

The bas-reliefs in the corners by Bela Lyon Pratt are the same as those in the Pavilion of the Discoverers. Only here they have Latin instead of English titles: *Ver* or Spring, *Aestas* or Summer, *Auctumnus* or Autumn, *Hiems* or Winter.

Robert Leftwich Dodge's Paintings

Each of the four lunettes is devoted to a single Element: the east lunette to Earth, the north to Air, the west to Fire, and the south to Water. The composition, which is very simple, is uniform throughout. In the middle of the lunette is a group of three figures typifying the subject of the decoration—the central figure standing and the other two seated. The latter are of women, but to prevent monotony, the standing figures are alternately male and female—male in the lunettes of Earth and Fire, and female in those of Air and Water. The central figure holds up in either hand an end of a heavy garland of flowers, which, stretching in a single festoon to the extremity of the lunette, is there caught up by a little boy. In the middle of each half of the picture, and in each lunette the same on both sides, is an ornamental bronze column flanked on either hand by a bronze standard or tripod, all three united by floating streamers or ribands into a single group, and each serving as a pedestal on which to place some emblems of the Element represented.

In the lunette of Earth the idea is the fertility and bounteousness of the soil. In the central group the figure to the right leans her arm upon an amphora or ancient wine jar and holds in her hand a rose. The figure to the left is that of a reaper, with a wreath of grains on her head and a bundle of wheat by her side, and holding in her hand a sickle. The boys at the ends of the decoration are dancing for jollity. The background is a smiling and luxuriant summer landscape, the fruits of which—the peach, the plum, the pear, the grape, and the rest—are displayed in the great garlands which the central figure holds up with outstretched arms. The bronze columns support baskets of fruit, and on the accompanying standards are perched magnificent peacocks. The border of the decoration includes masks, urns, and lions, the last emblematic of the

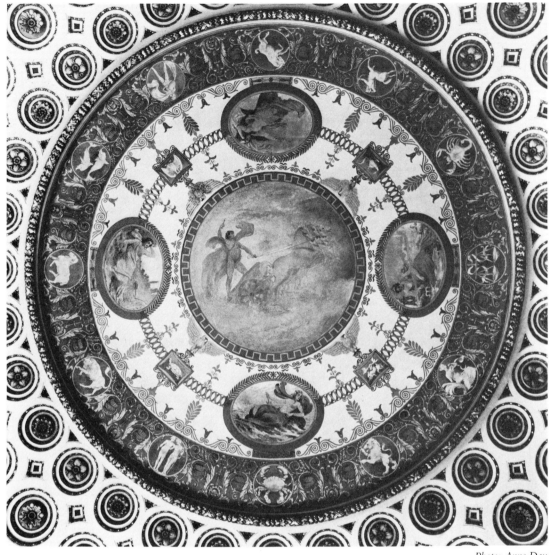

Apollo, the sun god, on his chariot in the center surrounded by eight ovals and medallions depicting the Four Elements, the whole encircled by a band with the signs of the Zodiac. By Elmer Ellsworth Garnsey. In the Southeast Pavilion or Pavilion of the Elements on the second floor.

subject of the decoration. Beneath the lunette of Earth are the names of Demeter, Hera, and Dionysus.

The central figure in the decoration typifying Air stands upon a bank of clouds; she is winged, and a large star blazes on her forehead. Of the figures to her right and left, the first is winged and the second carries the caduceus. The festoons are of morning glories, upheld at the further ends by flying cherubs. The background is sky and clouds. The central standards carry astrolabes, as being the typical astronomical instrument of a few centuries ago, and eagles are perched on those to the side. In the border, winged

145

griffins are substituted for lions. Under Air are tablets bearing the names of Hermes, Zeus, and Iris.

The background of the third lunette, Fire, is a mountainous and volcanic region, its peaks touched with lurid light from constant eruptions. The festoons are composed of sunflowers, and the seated figures in the center carry each a flaming torch. The columns to the right and left bear flaming globes, while the flanking standards support the fiery nest of the phoenix—the bird which was fabled by the ancients to live, sole of its species, five hundred years, at the end of which time it repaired to the desert and built a funeral pyre, in the flames of which it was consumed. From its ashes as a nest a new phoenix arose, as here depicted. In the border of the decoration are salamanders, which, according to the old superstition, lived in the midst of fire. The lunette of Fire is identified with the names of Hestia, Hephaistos, and Prometheus.

In the last lunette, Water, the central figure, clad in green, holds festoons of seaweed and water lilies—flowers, buds, and pads. On either side is a mermaid, one of them with a seashell. The background is the open sea. The standards are in the form of rostral columns (such as the Romans erected in honor of their victorious admirals) ornamented with garlands of laurel and the beaks and sterns of captured ships. On top is set a galley, with oars and sails. Over each of the standards to the side hovers a sea gull. The boys at the end of the picture have tails like mermaids, and in the border are dolphins. The tablets beneath the lunette of Water bear the names of Proteus, Galatea, and Poseidon.

The disc of the ceiling repeats in another form the general idea of the decorations of the lunettes. In the center is the sun, across which the sun god, Apollo, drives his four-horse chariot. The sun, however, is still the sun, and not a yellow background; the dusky picture outlined against it is to be taken as a vision, so to say, of its attributes.

Around the sun as a center is painted a chain of alternate medallions and cartouches—four of each, or eight in all—which typify the Four Elements represented in the lunettes below. A medallion and a cartouche are devoted to each. The former sort are painted so as to suggest a cameo design. The first of them, which occurs, like the other three, on the side nearest the lunette of the corresponding subject, typifies Earth, a female figure reclined amidst a summer landscape. In her hand is a scythe, and behind her is a plow, standing in the midst of a wheat field. Water is a mermaid riding off a rocky shore on the back of a dolphin. In her hand she holds an oar. Fire is a woman watching the smoke which floats away from the flame of a little brazier at her side. Behind her is a tripod on which incense is burning. In the distance is Mount Vesuvius, sending out a steady cloud of smoke, and in the plain beneath are the ruins of Pompeii. Air is a female figure clad in flowing drapery, and floating among the clouds on the outstretched wings of an eagle.

The cartouches are more simply designed. That of Earth contains a tortoise, on the back of which, according to the Hindu mythology, the earth is ultimately supported. Air is typified by a swan; Fire, by a lamp; and Water by two intertwined dolphins. Finally the whole decoration is surrounded by a broad band of arabesque ornament, in which are placed the signs of the Zodiac.

THE NORTHWEST GALLERY

The visitor retraces his steps to the Main Entrance Hall and proceeds north along the West Second-Floor Corridor to the Northwest Gallery.

At either end, occupying the same position as Kenyon Cox's decorations, and of the same size and shape, is a painting by Gari Melchers, illustrating, at the north, War, and at the south, Peace. The same subjects, it is interesting to note, were chosen by Melchers for his decorations at the World's Columbian Exposition of 1893 in Chicago. The present paintings may be taken, therefore, as representing the development and completion of a favorite idea of the artist.

Gari Melchers's Paintings

In the panel of War, the scene represented is that of a chieftain of some primitive tribe returning home with his clansmen across a desolate tract of open country from a successful battle. He is crowned with a wreath of laurel, and sits proudly astride a magnificent white horse. A second horseman rides beside him, and another a little behind. Three men carry a roughly constructed bier on which they

147

are bringing home the dead body of a warrior for burial in his native soil. In the righthand corner a woman kneels to care for a wounded man who has just sunk exhausted to the ground. Behind, a trumpeter sounds his horn, exulting in this dearly bought victory. To the left two foot soldiers carry shields emblazoned with devices of primitive heraldry. One of them holds on a leash two straining bloodhounds, eager for their kennels, and leading the way toward home.

Melchers's other painting, Peace, represents an early religious procession. The inhabitants of some little village, perhaps in prehistoric Greece, have come to the border of a grove bearing the image of their tutelar goddess, a small seated figure set on a little platform covered with an embroidered cloth. The procession has halted, and the priest is reading from a paper which he holds in his hand, containing, very likely, a blessing in the name of the goddess upon the fields and orchards of the villagers. Various objects, one of them the model of a ship, are carried in the procession to be offered up as memorials in the temple of the goddess, and in the rear a boy leads to the sacrifice a bull wreathed with garlands.

Names—forming a list of the world's most famous generals and admirals—were once inscribed in tablets above the doors and windows of the gallery: Cyrus, Alexander, Hannibal, Caesar, Charles Martel, William the Conqueror, Frederick the Great, Charlemagne, Eugene, Marlborough, Napoleon, Wellington, Nelson, Washington, Jackson, Scott, Grant, Farragut, Sherman, and Sheridan. They will be restored.

THE NORTHWEST PAVILION, THE NORTH GALLERY, AND THE NORTHEAST PAVILION

The Pavilion of Art and Science—William de Leftwich Dodge's Paintings

The entablature and paired pilasters which decorate the walls of the two pavilions to the south, are resumed in the Northwest Pavilion, or Pavilion of Art and Science, if one choose to name it, as the three corresponding rooms on this floor were named, from the subject of the paintings which it contains.

These paintings, both in the lunettes and in the ceiling disc, are the work of William de Leftwich Dodge. The

Ambition, *the ceiling mural of the Northwest Pavilion or Pavilion of Art and Science on the second floor. The Unattainable Ideal on a winged horse above those striving for success. William de Leftwich Dodge, painter.*

subjects are as follows: in the west lunette, Literature; north lunette, Music; east lunette, Science; south lunette, Art; and in the ceiling disc, Ambition, considered as the incentive of all human effort, whether in art, science, or affairs. Comparing them with the other decorations in the Library, the visitor will be struck with the unusually large number of figures which Dodge has introduced into his canvases, all, of course, helping to illustrate some phase of the subject under which they are grouped. Throughout, however, the meaning is unusually clear, the special significance of every figure being indicated either by some expressive attitude or action, or by the introduction of some appropriate and typical object.

Literature shows a varied group of male and female figures sitting or standing. The scene is along the steps of an old Greek temple. The God of Letters—or Apollo, if one wishes—sits in the foreground holding an open book. Behind him is a company of maidens reading in an ancient scroll, which they unroll from hand to hand. To the right, a woman is instructing two children in the rudiments of learning. Comedy, a nude and easy figure, is looking at

149

the ludicrous features of a comic mask, and Tragedy stands in an attitude of recitation, lifting her arms in an emphasizing gesture. In the corner is a little boy working over an ancient hand press. To the left a poet sits with his head bowed in thought, perhaps in despair that his verses have not received their due meed of applause; but Fame stands behind him holding out the wreath of laurel with which, after many years, she means to crown him. Further on is another poet, who, as he reclines half dreaming on the ground, is suddenly inspired with the rapture of the Muse. In the corner is a bust of Homer, with a pile of books for pedestal. Beneath Literature the names of the following countries are found on plaques: Greece, Italy, and England.

In Music, Apollo, as the God of Song and Harmony, is seated in the center of a long marble bench and is playing upon a lyre. Other figures, variously disposed throughout the panel, play upon a number of different musical instruments, illustrating at once the development and present scope of the art. One plays a violin, two others are blowing trumpets, a fourth has the double pipes, another a mandolin—and so on. The names of three cities are inscribed on tablets beneath Music: Venice, Berlin, and Paris.

The central figure of Science—the background of which is again the columns and marble steps of a temple—is a winged female figure descending through the air to crown the inventor of the phonograph, who kneels on the steps before her with a simple electrical instrument beside him. More broadly considered, the group typifies the triumphs of modern electrical science, summed up, indeed, in the invention of the phonograph, but including as well the electric telegraph and the telephone. To the right is a man holding the model of a propeller steamship, and further on a husbandman with his team of horses, gathering the fruits of Agriculture. To the left is a table on which are set two alembics for Physics and around which is gathered a group of scientists, one holding a human skull, which forms the subject of their discussion. The group may be taken to represent the various medical and surgical sciences, such as Physiology, Anatomy, and so forth. Further to the left is a figure looking at a kite lying on the ground—a reminder of Benjamin Franklin's famous electrical experiment with the kite and the key. In the background is a little campfire over which a teakettle is suspended, for Watt's celebrated discovery of the power of steam. Three cities are named beneath Science: Babylon, Tyre, and Carthage.

Art shows a student sketching a nude model. Behind him is his instructor criticizing his work. Sculpture is symbolized to the left, and, to the right, a young woman is painting a design upon a great Greek vase. Behind her are the capitals of a number of the more familiar orders of Architecture, as the Egyptian and the Ionic. Beneath Art are inscribed the names of three cities: Thebes, Athens, and Rhodes.

In the painting of Ambition in the ceiling, the scene is supposed to be the top of a high mountain, but only the marble terrace which marks the summit is actually visible in the painting. Here is gathered a group which has toiled along a weary path up the mountainside to comparative success; but none is satisfied. Above them, the Unattainable Ideal, a figure holding aloft in mockery the palm branch of complete achievement, rides through the air on a great winged horse. In front is Fame, grasping the horse's bridle with one hand, and turning to those below to sound a derisive note on her trumpet. The figures on the mountaintop are involved in a scene of mad confusion; some for the moment are distracted by crime or lust, or cynical contempt, but most reach out their arms in ineffectual eagerness to attain the glorious vision above them. They have leapt to the top of the terrace in their fierce desire to gain the slightest advantage. To the left, a murderer shrinks back in horror from the body of the miser whom he has just slain; as he starts away, aghast at his crime, he topples over a flaming tripod which had been set on a post of the terrace. Conspicuous figures in the mad struggle for success are a warrior, with sword, greaves, and helmet, and a sculptor, bearing a statuette of the Venus of Milo. In front of them is the seated figure of a poet, with a bandage over his eyes to indicate the abstraction and ideality of his thought. Further on, a man flings out both arms in a mad appeal and, on the moment, is grasped in the arms of a woman, who drags him back to the level of her own baseness. A jester, one of Shakespeare's fools, in his cap and particolored coat, stands near by, holding a bauble surmounted by a skull in one hand, and a statuette of Victory in the other. That fame comes only after death, and that the promptings of personal ambition are but a hollow mockery, is the moral that he preaches.

In the four corners beneath the ceiling are the round reliefs symbolizing the Four Seasons. The work of Bela Lyon Pratt they are the same as those found in the Southwest and Southeast Pavilions.

THE NORTH GALLERY LINKS THE NORTHWEST AND NORTHEAST PAVILIONS

The Pavilion of the Seals—William Brantley Van Ingen's Paintings and Elmer Ellsworth Garnsey's Ceiling Painting

The fourth of the pavilions in the Pavilion of the Seals, at the northeast corner of the building. The walls in this room, it may be noted, are treated differently from those of the other three pavilions. Instead of the frieze and the paired pilasters, one has wall surfaces covered with gilding and ornamented with painted laurel bands arranged in regular patterns recalling the designs of the parterres of an old-fashioned garden.

The paintings in the lunettes are by William Brantley Van Ingen, and illustrate the seals of the various executive departments of the United States government. The disc of the domed ceiling was designed by Elmer Ellsworth Garnsey, and shows the Great Seal of the United States surrounded by allegorical emblems.

As in the previous pavilions on this floor, the general arrangement of the decoration is the same in all four lunettes. In each the artist has introduced a low terrace or wall of masonry running from end to end, thus serving both to ballast the picture, as it were, and to bind its parts more strongly together. A recess in the center of the terrace allows space for a circular tablet, painted to represent wood, about 6 feet in diameter, or nearly the height of the lunette. On this are inscribed, as if in raised letters, one or more quotations from the writings or speeches of great American statesmen. These were selected by the librarian, Ainsworth Rand Spofford, mainly for their general patriotic application, but, of course, as far as possible with some special reference to the subject of the decoration. The border of each tablet, as of the decoration itself, is a band of laurel leaves, suggested by the laurel roll which outlines the disc of the ceiling.

On either side of the tablet is a female figure, seated against the terrace, personifying a department of the government, in token of which she supports a shield or cartouche on which the seal of that Department is conspicuously displayed. The visitor will notice that these figures (in this respect like Robert Reid's in the North Second-Floor Corridor) illustrate the American type of woman, and wear modern gowns and not conventional Greek or Roman drapery.

The two figures and the tablet between form the necessary central pyramidal composition. For a limit and balance to the decoration the artist has painted, at either end, a cypress tree and, in all but one of the lunettes, one or two cherubs, usually engaged in some action which shall be useful in explaining the purport of the picture, the meaning of which is still further brought out, in most cases, by introducing into the background a well-known monument or building, or some conventional object, suggestive of the functions of the department represented.

The west lunette is devoted to the Department of the Treasury and the Department of State; the north lunette to the Department of Justice and the Post Office Department; the east lunette to the Departments of Agriculture and the Interior; and the south lunette to the War and Navy Departments.

Half a lunette is devoted to each. The Department of the Treasury—to begin with the one first named in the above list—is sufficiently indicated by the introduction of the Treasury Building in the background. Two children are playing on the parapet, one of them with his foot on a strongbox. The background of the other portion of the lunette—illustrating the Department of State—exhibits the dome and west front of the Capitol and, to the right, the Washington Monument. The vital thing about a nation—that which it is the first business of a Department of State to help preserve—is its independence. The Monument may be taken, therefore, as standing for the establishment of that independence, and the Capitol for its maintenance. A dog, typical of fidelity, lies in the foreground. The cypress trees, it may be noted before passing to the next lunette, are introduced purely for their decorative effect, and are without any symbolic meaning. In all the decorations they are set in jars copied from Zuñi originals in the National Museum of Natural History.

In the north lunette, the figure of Justice is clad in ermine. On the terrace is a high bronze standard, carrying a pair of evenly balanced scales. The boy at the left holds a measuring rod, for exact justice. In the other half of the painting, devoted to the Post Office Department, the boy is represented with a pair of compasses marking out mail routes on a globe. Mercury was the messenger of the gods, according to classic mythology, and a bronze statue of him with his winged sandals, staff, and cap, is appropriately set upon the stone terrace to typify the dispatch and celerity of the Department.

Agriculture, in the next lunette, is symbolized solely in the fertile and well-cultivated landscape which forms the background of her portion of the decoration. The chief duty of the Department of the Interior—to protect and control the Indians—is indicated in the background of the other half of the picture by a representation of the curious method of burial, if one may use the word, which prevails among certain of the western tribes—the body, lashed to a few poles for a bier, being laid away in the branches of a tree.

In the last lunette, that of War and the Navy, the terrace is nicked and shattered by the bullets of the enemy. The figure to the left, representing the Department of War, holds a regulation army sword, and the figure to the right a naval sword. To the left the two boys are engaged in combat; one is falling, stained with blood, while the other presses upon him with a falchion, or Roman sword. The corresponding composition to the right is much the same; the chief difference being the trident which the victor aims at his opponent's breast. War is accompanied by a Roman standard adapted to an American use by altering the old initials "S.P.Q.R."—"The Senate and People of Rome"—to "U.S.A." In the background is Bunker Hill Monument in Boston. On the other side are the masts of the battleship *Indiana,* and a rostral column of the same sort as those used in the lunette representing Water in the Pavilion of the Elements, but in this case copied exactly from the one erected in honor of Commodore Decatur and afterward removed to Annapolis, where it is now. The inscriptions on the tablets in the four lunettes may most conveniently be inserted here. In the west lunette, that of the State and Treasury Departments, the quotations are as follows:

'Tis our true policy to steer clear of permanent alliance with any portion of the foreign world.   —Washington

Let our object be our country, our whole country, and nothing but our country.   —Webster

Thank God I also am an American.   —Webster

In the north lunette:

Equal and exact justice to all men, of whatever state or persuasion, religious or political: peace, commerce and honest friendship with all nations—entangling alliance with none.
     —Thomas Jefferson

In the east lunette:

The agricultural interest of the country is connected with every other, and superior in importance to them all.
     —Andrew Jackson

Let us have peace.   —U. S. Grant

In the south lunette:

The aggregate happiness of society is, or ought to be, the end of all government.   —Washington

To be prepared for war is one of the most effective means of preserving peace.   —Washington

The disc of the dome, by Elmer Ellsworth Garnsey, contains one of the most interesting and ingeniously arranged of the purely conventional decorations which ornament the Library. In the center is the great seal of the United States, which puts the final touch of significance upon the series of paintings in the lunettes. Surrounding it is a circular band containing forty-eight stars which then constituted the United States, one for each State and Territory. On the diagonal axes of the room are four medallions containing heads symbolizing the Four Winds— North, South, East, and West—each blowing a gale from his mouth, as in the classical representations. They stand, of course, for the four great natural divisions of the country. Below each medallion is a garland of fruits or grains, festooned from bunches of eagles' feathers which spring from the central panel of the decoration, and indicating the nature of the products of each section. The garland under the medallion of the North Wind, for example, is composed of apples, pears, peaches, and similar fruits; that under the East Wind, of various vegetables and berries; under the West Wind, grains, as wheat, oats, and maize; and under the South Wind, bananas, pomegranates, oranges, lemons, and so forth.

Other emblematic objects introduced into the decoration are lyres, each flanked on either side by a horn of plenty filled with fruits; and flaming torches, set between a pair of dolphins. There are thus two sorts of groups, each of which occurs four times in the decoration in accordance with the standard fixed by the four medallions of the Winds. The four different objects depicted signify four of the great interests of the country—the lyre, the Fine Arts; the cornucopia, Agriculture; the torch, Learning and Education; and the dolphin, Maritime Commerce. Finally the composition is united by American flags festooned from the lyres to the garlands of fruit which underhang the medallions of the Winds. And around the whole is a narrow border, on which are inscribed the following words from Lincoln's Gettysburg Address, used also, in part, by Elihu Vedder in his decorations in the first lobby of the Rotunda Reading Room

> That this nation, under God, shall have a new birth of freedom; that government of the people, by the people, for the people, shall not perish from the earth.

Here, as in the other three Pavilions, Bela Lyon Pratt's circular reliefs symbolizing the Four Seasons are found in the four corners between the lunettes.

OTHER ROOMS IN THE BUILDING

The Whittall Pavilion

Off the North Corridor of the basement floor is the Whittall Pavilion with a courtyard garden. It was given in 1938 by Gertrude Clarke Whittall of Washington to house the Stradivarius violins which she had donated three years previously. Other musical instruments, subsequently given the Library, are also kept here.

The Coolidge Auditorium

Beyond the Whittall Pavilion, on the same side of the corridor, is the Coolidge Auditorium with a seating capacity of 511. Given by Elizabeth Sprague Coolidge of Chicago, the auditorium was specially built in 1925 for chamber-music recitals. Charles Adams Platt, architect of the Freer Gallery of Art, was the designer.

On the Second Street or east side of the building, on the second floor, are the Rare Book and Special Collections Reading Room and the Hispanic Reading Room, easily reached by elevator on the same side of the building.

The Rare Book and Special Collections Reading Room

The Rare Book Room is entered by elaborate bronze doors consisting of panels framed with classical detail. On the lefthand door the top panel bears the device of Johann Fust and Peter Schoeffer of Mainz, Germany, who were the associates of Johann Gutenberg in introducing printing to the Western world. Below this appears the emblem of Geoffroy Tory, French calligrapher and designer of the sixteenth century. The bottom panel shows the printer's mark of William Morris, founder in 1891 of the Kelmscott Press in England, which did much to revive the art of fine printing. On the righthand door the panel at the top contains the names of Juan Cromberger and Juan Pablos, founder and first printer, respectively, of the earliest press to operate in the New World, established in Mexico City in 1539. In the center panel are the names of Stephen Daye, who had the first press in what was to become the United States—that is, in Cambridge, Massachusetts, in 1639— William Nuthead, founder of the first Virginia and first Maryland presses, and William Bradford, who brought the first presses to New York and Philadelphia. The last panel reproduces the device most usually associated with the name of the late Bruce Rogers, distinguished American designer of types and books.

The Rare Book and Special Collections Reading Room was built in 1935. Its design was inspired by a room in Independence Hall, Philadelphia.

At the south end of the corridor is the Hispanic Society Reading Room. Its vestibule and north end are decorated with murals executed in 1941 by the Brazilian artist Candido Portinari. Done in tempera paints on plaster walls the subjects are the Discovery of the New World, Pioneering the Forests of the New World, Missionaries Teaching the Indians, and Gold Mining.

The Hispanic Society Reading Room

157

The main room, with a barrel vault, is the work of the Philadelphia architect Paul Philippe Cret. Opened in 1939, it is in the classical *Siglo de Oro* Style of sixteenth- and seventeenth-century Spain and Portugal. Around the walls is a dado of blue tiles from Pueblo, Mexico. Over the windows and the doors leading to the stacks are panels with the names of historic and literary figures of Hispanic origin: Camões, Cervantes, Bello, Medina, Cuervo, Palmo, Dario, Gonçalves Dias, Sarmiento, Hostos, Montalvo, Rodó, García Icazbalceta, and Heredia.

A marble tablet, elaborately framed, commemorates the gift of the room to the Library:

THE HISPANIC FOUNDATION

IN

THE LIBRARY OF CONGRESS

THIS CENTER

FOR THE PURPOSE OF STUDIES

IN SPANISH, PORTUGUESE AND LATIN-AMERICAN CULTURE

HAS BEEN ESTABLISHED

WITH THE GENEROUS COOPERATION OF

THE HISPANIC SOCIETY OF AMERICA

IN EXTENSION

OF ITS SERVICE TO LEARNING

MCMXXXVIII

In 1940 a mural painted on stainless steel was given to the Library by the Allegheny Ludlum Steel Corporation of Pittsburgh. Executed by Mrs. Buell Mullen of Chicago and placed above the marble tablet, it depicts the arms of Christopher Columbus with the inscription:

POR CASTILLA Y LEÓN

NUEVO MONDO HALLÓ COLÓN

(For Castille and for León, Columbus Founded a New World)

With the continuing and ever-mounting flood of printed matter, to which have been added copies of movies, records, tapes, and so forth, an annex to the main building was inevitable. In 1938 the John Adams Building, designed by Pierson & Wilson, with Alexander Buel Trowbridge as consulting architect, was completed and opened to the public. It has been described as "essentially a solid mass of shelving encircled with work spaces." In style it is "Art Deco," which is to say that its ornament was inspired by the Exposition des Arts Décoratifs held in Paris in 1925.

Sculpture by Lee Lawrie is to be found on the building's bronze doors. The center doors at the west entrance, on Second Street, have six figures. They consist of the following: Mercury or Hermes, the messenger of the gods; Odin, the Viking-Germanic god of war and creator of the runic alphabet; Ogma, the Irish god who invented the Gaelic alphabet; Itzama, god of the Mayans; Quetzalcoatl, the god of the Aztecs; and Sequoyah, an American Indian. They are represented here because they are presumed to have encouraged written communication. The same panels are to be found on the flanking doors of the east entrance on Third Street.

The flanking doors of the west entrance have six other personages who are part of the history of the written world. They are Thoth, an Egyptian god; Ts'ang Chieh, the Chinese patron of writing; Nabu Sumero, an Akkadian god; Brahma, the Indian god; the Greek Cadmus, the sower of dragon's teeth; and Tahmurath, a hero of the ancient Persians. These same figures are to be seen on the center door of the east entrance.

On the south side of the building, on Independence Avenue, there is only one door. Of the two figures here, one, male, represents physical labor beneath the seal of the United States, and the other, female, stands for intellectual labor, beneath an open book surrounded by a laurel wreath.

Inside, two reading rooms on the fifth floor have decorations by the artist Ezra Winter. The Thomas Jefferson Reading Room North, has two large murals devoted to the Canterbury Pilgrims, those which figure in Chaucer's *Canterbury Tales*. In addition, a small rectangle above a clock has for its subject the Prologue of the *Tales,* which

159

begins "When that Aprille with his shoures soote . . ." There is also a lunette with three musicians, "Thise olde gentile Britouns in hir dayes . . . ," inspired by the Prologue of the *Franklin's Tale.* In the south room, the Science Reading Room, Winter executed two large panels, 60 feet long and 6 feet high, devoted to Freedom, Labor, Education, and Democratic Government. The rectangle over the clock is dedicated to "the living generation," while the lunette opposite has a portrait of Thomas Jefferson with his residence, Monticello, in the background.

THE JAMES MADISON MEMORIAL BUILDING

The latest addition to the Library of Congress is the second annex called the James Madison Memorial Building with its entrance on Independence Avenue. It was completed in 1980 on the designs of DeWitt, Poor and Shelton, Associated Architects. Over the main entrance is a relief of books in bronze by Frank Eliscu. Off the Entrance Hall, to the immediate left, is the James Madison Memorial Hall, with a floor and piers of marble and walls of teak. At the end of it is a heroic statue of James Madison by Walker Hancock. Behind the statue is a two-story exhibition hall. At the end of the Entrance Hall is a pair of bronze medallions by Robert Alexander Weinmann. The one on the left shows the profile of James Madison and that on the right depicts Madison at work. The Entrance Hall leads to a central courtyard with a fountain by Robert M. Cronbach.

The style of the building is modern, as is the design of the fountain.

APPENDICES

The glossary consists of two parts: photographs of different parts of the building with the elements and ornament labeled, and an illustrated list of definitions of terms.

The glossary was based on William R. Ware's *The American Vignola,* published in the Classical America Series in Art and Architecture. For those desiring further information on the classical vocabulary, the editor can only recommend that excellent book.

For help on the glossary the editor would like to thank Alan Burnham, James Parker of the Metropolitan Museum of Art, and Dr. Richard H. Howland of the Smithsonian Institution. The photographs are by Anne Day, and the drawings were executed by Harvey Heiser, Alvin Holm, and Cameron MacTavish.

—HHR

IONIC COLUMN, *identified by*
the pair of spiral volutes or scrolls of
its capital. This one is to be found
supporting an arch at the Main
Entrance.

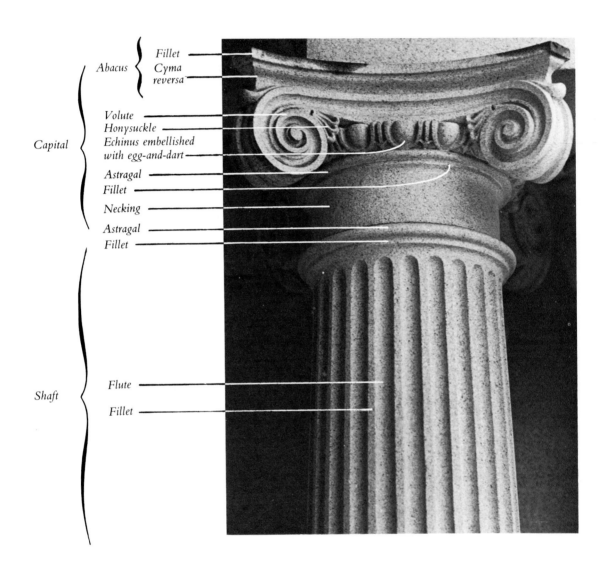

Abacus { *Fillet*
Cyma
reversa

Volute
Honysuckle
Echinus embellished
with egg-and-dart
Capital
Astragal
Fillet
Necking
Astragal
Fillet

Shaft
Flute
Fillet

164

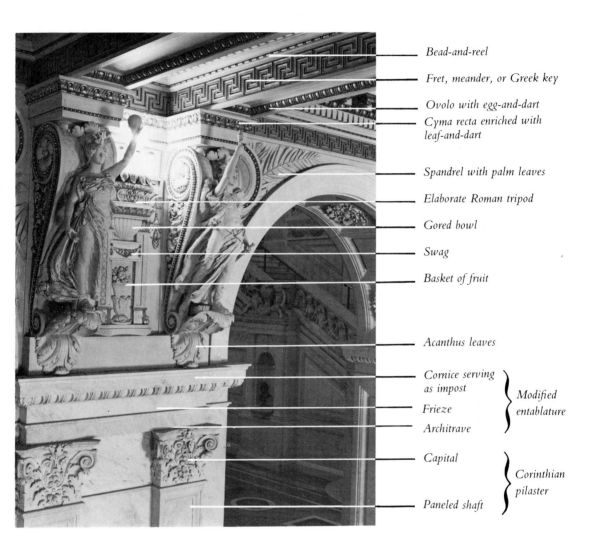

Decoration of the Vestibule at the Main Entrance with sculpture by Herbert Adams.

Bead-and-reel

Fret, meander, or Greek key

Ovolo with egg-and-dart

Cyma recta enriched with leaf-and-dart

Spandrel with palm leaves

Elaborate Roman tripod

Gored bowl

Swag

Basket of fruit

Acanthus leaves

Cornice serving as impost

Frieze ⎫ Modified entablature

Architrave ⎭

Capital ⎫ Corinthian pilaster

Paneled shaft ⎭

165

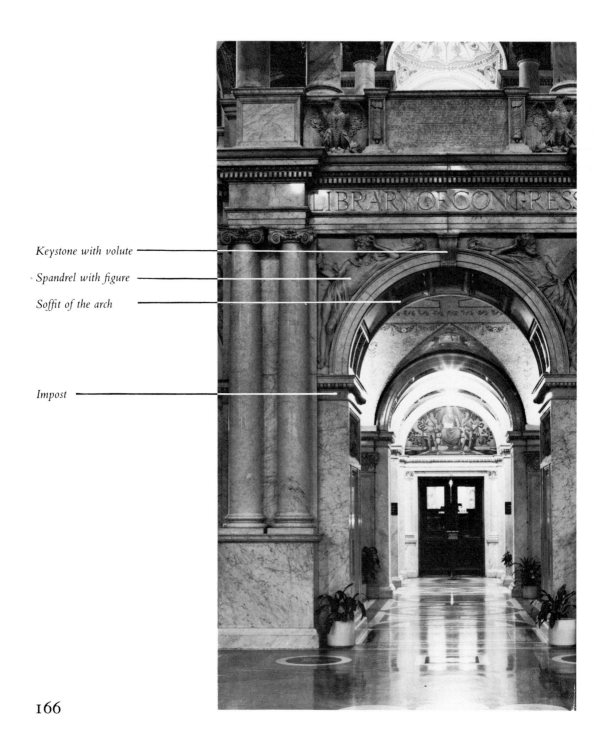

MEMORIAL ARCH *in the*
Main Entrance Hall leading to the
East Corridor and the Rotunda
Reading Room. The figures in the
spandrels, called "The Students," are
by Olin Levi Warner.

Keystone with volute

Spandrel with figure

Soffit of the arch

Impost

166

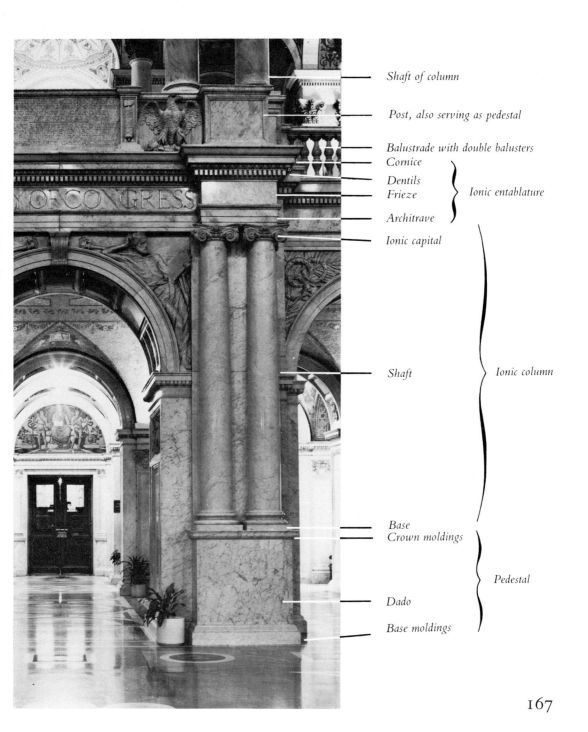

Shaft of column

Post, also serving as pedestal

Balustrade with double balusters
Cornice
Dentils
Frieze
Architrave

⎫
⎬ Ionic entablature
⎭

Ionic capital

Shaft

⎫
⎬ Ionic column
⎭

Base
Crown moldings

⎫
⎬ Pedestal
⎭

Dado

Base moldings

167

*Corner of the ceiling of the
Main Entrance Hall.*

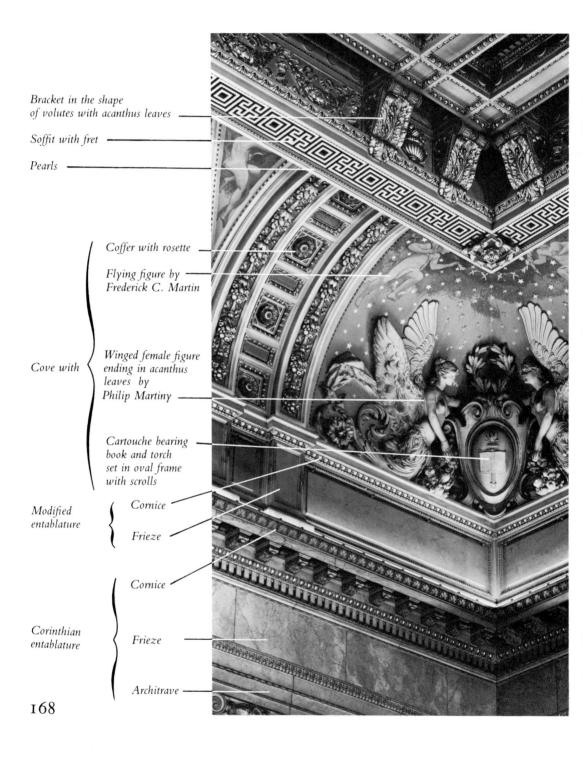

Bracket in the shape
of volutes with acanthus leaves

Soffit with fret

Pearls

Coffer with rosette

Flying figure by
Frederick C. Martin

Cove with

Winged female figure
ending in acanthus
leaves by
Philip Martiny

Cartouche bearing
book and torch
set in oval frame
with scrolls

Modified
entablature

Cornice

Frieze

Cornice

Corinthian
entablature

Frieze

Architrave

168

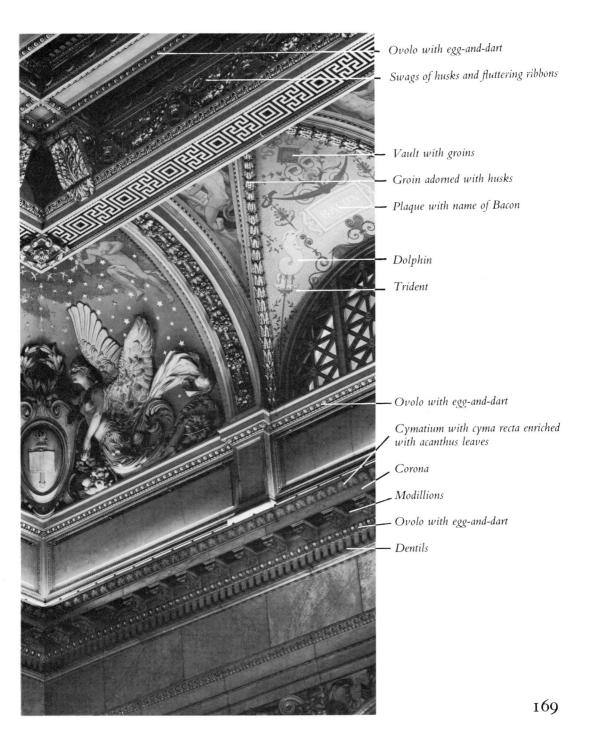

Ovolo with egg-and-dart

Swags of husks and fluttering ribbons

Vault with groins

Groin adorned with husks

Plaque with name of Bacon

Dolphin

Trident

Ovolo with egg-and-dart

Cymatium with cyma recta enriched with acanthus leaves

Corona

Modillions

Ovolo with egg-and-dart

Dentils

169

*North Corridor leading to the
Northwest Pavilion on the
first floor.*

Soffit of arch ————————

Saucer dome with coffers ——

Pendentive ————————

Corinthian
entablature ⎰ Cornice ————
⎱ Frieze ————
Architrave ——

Capital ————

Corinthian
pilaster ⎰ Shaft ————

Base ————

Pedestal ————————

Mosaic floor ————————

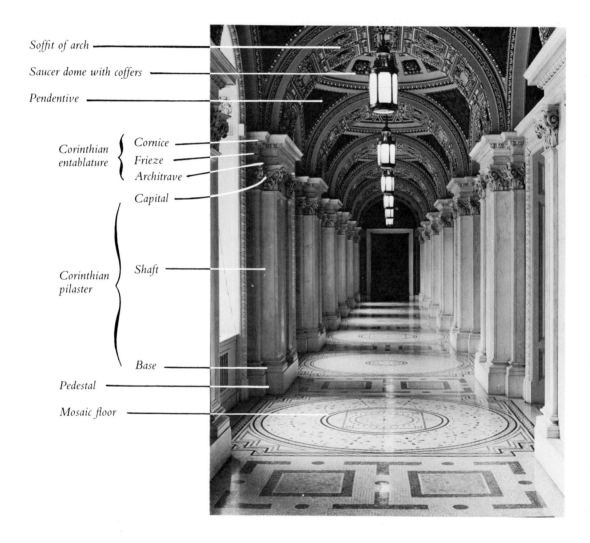

Soffit or underside of an arch in the North Corridor of the first floor.

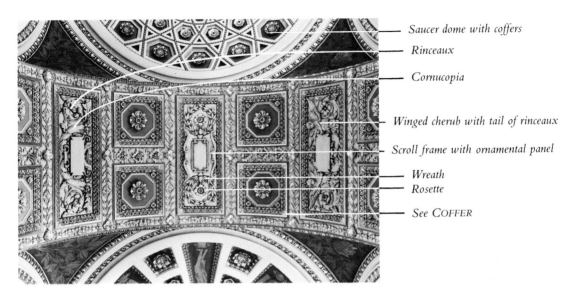

— Saucer dome with coffers
— Rinceaux
— Cornucopia

— Winged cherub with tail of rinceaux
— Scroll frame with ornamental panel
— Wreath
— Rosette
— See COFFER

Coffer on the soffit of an arch in the North Corridor of the first floor.

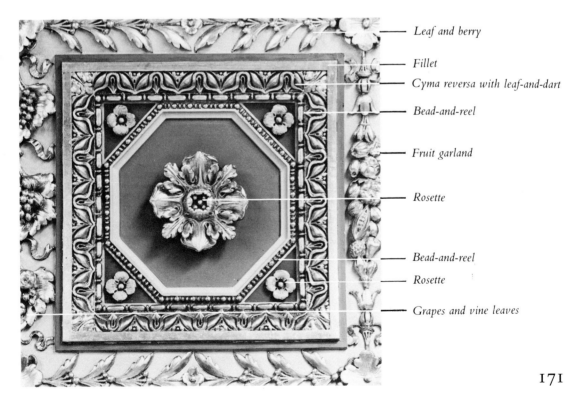

— Leaf and berry

— Fillet
— Cyma reversa with leaf-and-dart
— Bead-and-reel

— Fruit garland

— Rosette

— Bead-and-reel
— Rosette

— Grapes and vine leaves

171

Pendentive in the Librarian's Room.

Dome with urns, fluttering
ribbons, and bay-leaf swags

Cavetto with acanthus leaves

Rosettes with fluttering ribbons

Fruit garlands

Pearls

Bead-and-reel

Spray of bay leaves and bayberries

Egg-and-dart

American eagle above the fireplace in the Council of Scholars Reading Room.

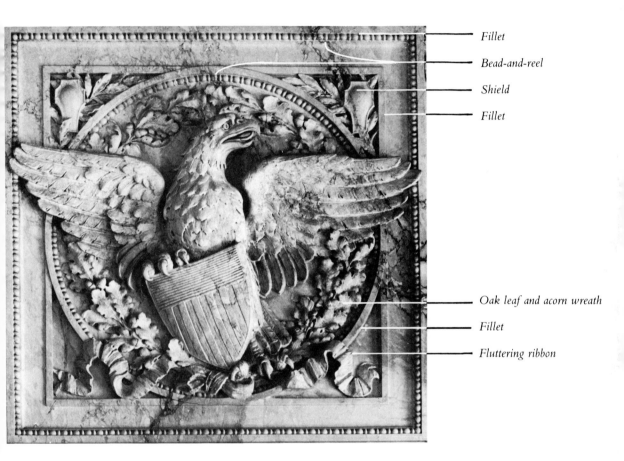

Fillet

Bead-and-reel

Shield

Fillet

Oak leaf and acorn wreath

Fillet

Fluttering ribbon

Corinthian entablature and capital in the Rotunda Reading Room.

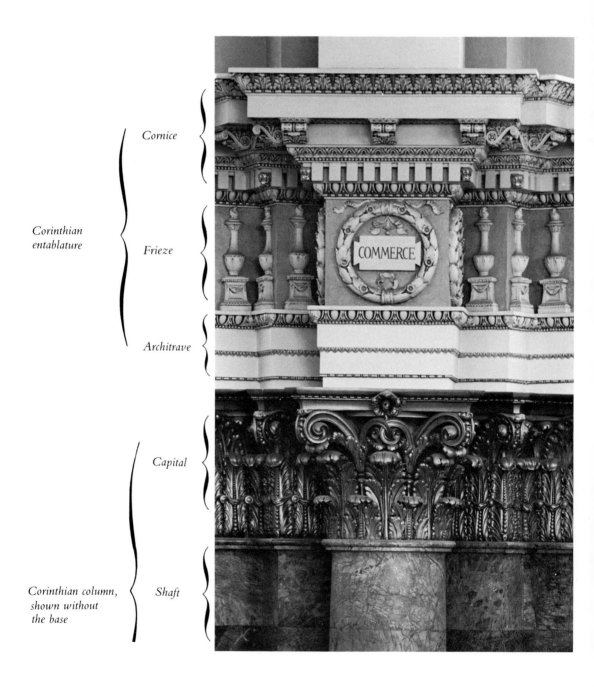

Cornice

Corinthian entablature

Frieze

COMMERCE

Architrave

Capital

Corinthian column, shown without the base

Shaft

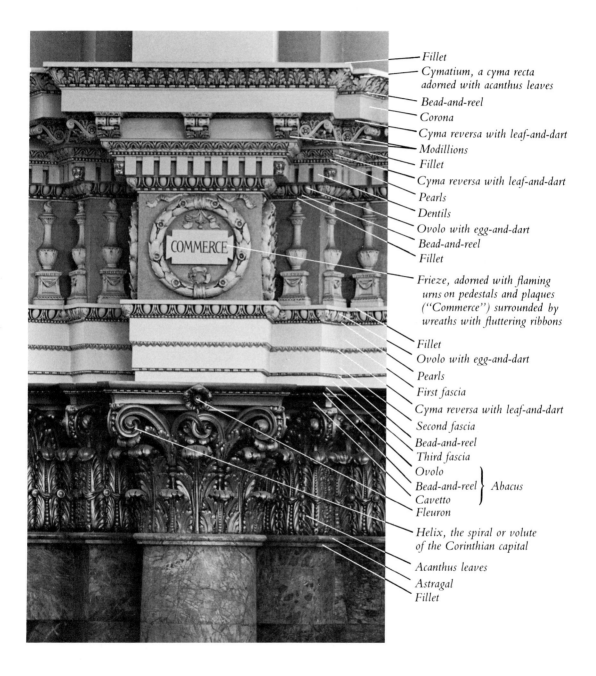

Fillet

Cymatium, a cyma recta
adorned with acanthus leaves

Bead-and-reel

Corona

Cyma reversa with leaf-and-dart

Modillions

Fillet

Cyma reversa with leaf-and-dart

Pearls

Dentils

Ovolo with egg-and-dart

Bead-and-reel

Fillet

Frieze, adorned with flaming
urns on pedestals and plaques
("Commerce") surrounded by
wreaths with fluttering ribbons

Fillet

Ovolo with egg-and-dart

Pearls

First fascia

Cyma reversa with leaf-and-dart

Second fascia

Bead-and-reel

Third fascia

Ovolo

Bead-and-reel ⎫
⎬ Abacus
Cavetto ⎭

Fleuron

Helix, the spiral or volute
of the Corinthian capital

Acanthus leaves

Astragal

Fillet

175

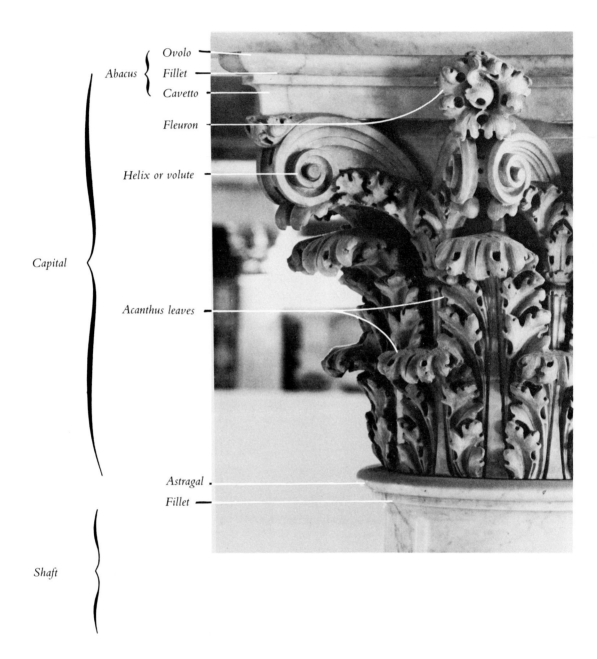

Corinthian capital on the second-floor colonnade around the Main Entrance Hall.

Abacus { Ovolo
Fillet
Cavetto

Fleuron

Helix or volute

Capital

Acanthus leaves

Astragal
Fillet

Shaft

176

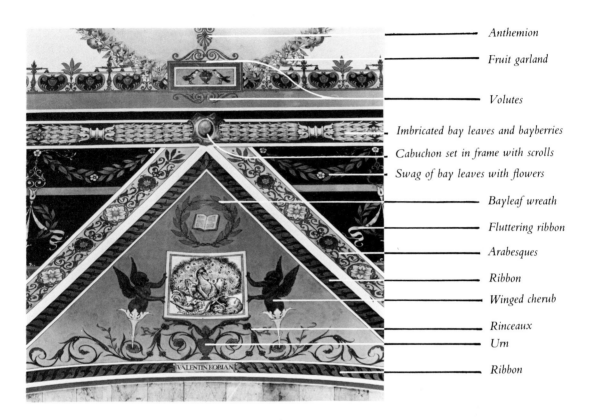

Anthemion

Fruit garland

Volutes

Imbricated bay leaves and bayberries

Cabuchon set in frame with scrolls

Swag of bay leaves with flowers

Bayleaf wreath

Fluttering ribbon

Arabesques

Ribbon

Winged cherub

Rinceaux

Urn

Ribbon

Balustrade with double balusters on
the second-floor corridors around the
Main Entrance Hall.

Upper rail ——————————

Abacus ——————————

Ovolo ——————————
Fillet ——————————

Sleeve ——————————

Belly ——————————

Astragal ——————————

Belly ——————————

Sleeve ——————————

Fillet ——————————
Ovolo ——————————

Base ——————————

Lower rail ——————————

178

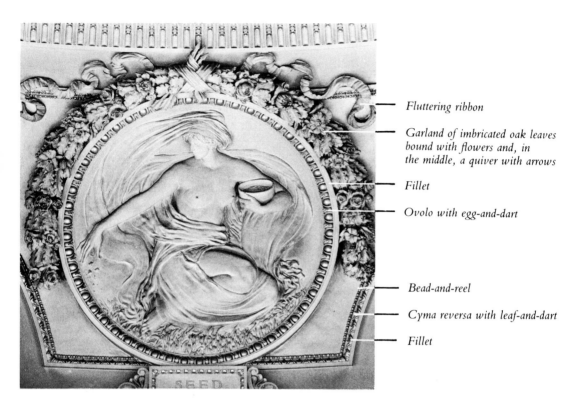

Fluttering ribbon

Garland of imbricated oak leaves bound with flowers and, in the middle, a quiver with arrows

Fillet

Ovolo with egg-and-dart

Bead-and-reel

Cyma reversa with leaf-and-dart

Fillet

179

Abacus. The slab that forms the top of the capital.

Acanthus. A Mediterranean plant (Acanthus mollis and Acanthus spinosus) whose deeply serrated leaf was stylized by the Greeks and Romans to become one of the principal ornaments of classical architecture. It identifies the Corinthian capital.

Acanthus Spinosus   *Acanthus*

Anthemion (anthemia, pl.). An ornament based on the honeysuckle or palmette.

Arabesque. An intricate decorative pattern joining plant, animal, and sometimes human forms.

Architrave. The bottom third of the entablature, the part resting on the column or pilaster and supporting the frieze. *See* ORDERS OF ARCHITECTURE.

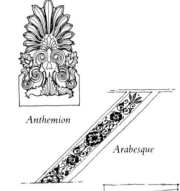

Anthemion

Arabesque

Astragal. A small half-round molding. *See* MOLDINGS.

Baluster. An upright support in a variety of turned shapes, customarily swelling toward its base. When one shape is inverted and superimposed on its model, it is called a *double baluster.* Used in a series and supporting a rail, it forms part of a *balustrade.*

Double Baluster

Balustrade

Base. The bottom part, made up of moldings, of the column and the pilaster, or of any architectural or decorative design. *See* ORDERS OF ARCHITECTURE.

Bay leaf. Also laurel leaf, the leaf of the bay tree or laurel tree (Laurus nobilis) used as an enrichment.

Bead-and-reel. A molding made up of beads separated by disks. *See* CORNICE.

Beads. *See* PEARLS.

Bed mold. The molding on which the top of a cornice rests.

Bay Leaf

Bead-and-Reel

181

Bracket

Cabuchon

Cartouche

Bracket. A support for a projection, such as a cornice, usually scroll-shaped as in a console bracket.

Cabuchon. A round or ovoid device with a convex surface, often elaborately framed. Also found in jewelry.

Capital. The crowning member of a column or a pilaster. *See* ORDERS OF ARCHITECTURE.

Cartouche. A shield or ovoid form often bearing inscriptions and devices in relief, frequently set in an elaborate scroll frame or surrounded with wreaths and garlands, as seen in the corner of the ceiling of the Main Entrance Hall.

Cavetto. A concave molding with the profile of a quarter-round or close to it. *See* MOLDINGS.

Coffer. A sunken panel in a ceiling, vault, or dome, or the underside of an arch. (Illustration shows coffers in a Dome.) The great example of coffering is to be found in the Pantheon in Rome.

Column. A round, vertical support, consisting of a base, shaft, and capital, usually upholding an entablature. *See* ORDERS OF architecture.

Corinthian column. One of the five orders, of columns mainly distinguished by its capital of acanthus leaves and volutes. It was the favorite order of the Romans. *See* ORDERS OF ARCHITECTURE, CORINTHIAN.

Cornice. The projecting top section of an entablature.

Cornice

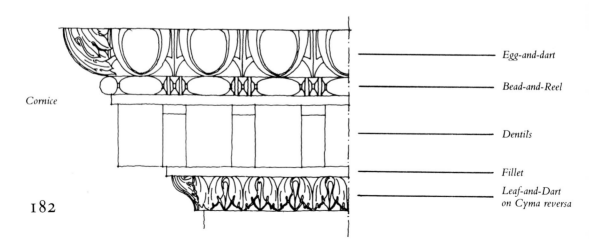

Egg-and-dart

Bead-and-Reel

Dentils

Fillet

Leaf-and-Dart on *Cyma reversa*

Cornucopia. Also known as a *horn of plenty,* it is a goat's horn overflowing with fruit, grain, ears of corn, and other items.

Corona. The flat part of a cornice between the cymatium above and the bed mold below.

Cove. A concave surface connecting a wall and a ceiling.

Cyma recta. A molding with an S-shaped curve, concave over convex. *See* Moldings.

Cyma reversa. A molding with an S-shaped curve, convex over concave. *See* Moldings.

Cymatium. The upper molding of a cornice, usually in the shape of a cyma recta.

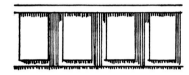

Dentil

Dentil. A small projecting block used in rows, called a dentil course, forming part of a cornice. Dentils resemble teeth. *Denticulated* or *Denticular* meaning enriched with dentils. *See* Cornice.

Dome. A convex roof or ceiling, hemispherical, semiovoidal, or saucer-shaped, built over a square, octagon, or circular space.

Dome

Echinus. An ovolo or quarter-round molding that is part of a capital. See Orders of architecture, Ionic.

Egg-and-dart. A familiar convex molding, an ovolo in profile enriched with eggs and arrowheads. *Also see* Cornice.

Egg-and-Dart

Entablature. The upper part of an order, above the column capitals. Made up of three major horizontal members: architrave, frieze, and cornice. *See* Orders of architecture.

Entasis. The slight curving of the shaft of a classical column to correct the optical illusion of concavity which results if the shaft is straight.

Fascia. The plain horizontal band or bands, often combined with molding, making up the architrave, the lowest, third part of the entablature. *See* Orders of architecture.

Festoon. A garland, made of fruits, flowers, leaves, or husks, and hanging in a curve. *Also see* Garland. Alternative term: Swag.

Festoon

Fillet. A raised, narrow flat band between the flutes of a column or as a raised band combined with other moldings. *See* Moldings.

183

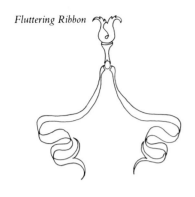

Fluttering Ribbon

Fluttering Ribbon

Garland

Imbrications

Leaf-and-Dart

Fleuron. A small flower-shaped ornament usually found on the abacus of a Corinthian column. *See* ORDERS OF ARCHITECTURE, CORINTHIAN.

Flute. A concave groove running vertically on a column or pilaster shaft. Collectively called fluting.

Fluttering ribbon. (See illustrations.)

Fret. A geometrical meandering pattern of horizontal and vertical straight lines making up a band. Also called *Greek key*. As seen on the ceiling of the Main Entrance Hall.

 *Fret*

Garland. An intertwining of fruits, flowers, leaves, or husks.

Gored. Cut into tapering forms.

Greek key. *See* FRET.

Groin. The intersection of two vaults.

Guilloche. An ornament composed of continuous interlaced curving lines. When there are two linked patterns, it is known as a double guilloche.

Double Guilloche   *Single Guilloche*

Helix. The volutes or scrolls of a Corinthian capital. *See* ORDERS OF ARCHITECTURE, CORINTHIAN.

Imbricated. The overlapping of bay leaves and bayberries, oak leaves and acorns, or coins. *Imbrication:* a band of the same.

Impost. A cornicelike bracket from which an arch springs.

Ionic. One of the five orders of columns recognized by its capital of volutes. *See* ORDERS OF ARCHITECTURE.

Keystone. The wedged top stone of an arch.

Leaf-and-dart. A repetitive band made up of a stylized leaf and a dart.

Meander. *See* FRET.

Metope. A square panel between triglyphs on a Doric frieze. *See* ORDER OF ARCHITECTURE, DORIC.

Modillion. A small bracket used in rows under the corona of a cornice and extending from the bed mold. It frequently takes the shape of an ornamental double volute.

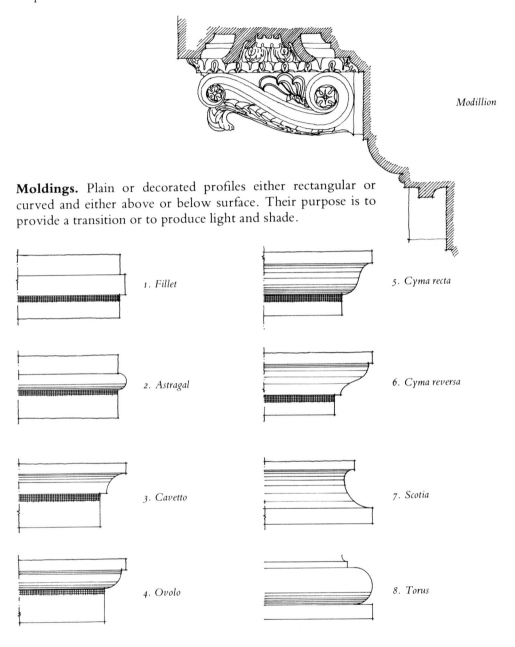

Modillion

Moldings. Plain or decorated profiles either rectangular or curved and either above or below surface. Their purpose is to provide a transition or to produce light and shade.

1. Fillet

5. Cyma recta

2. Astragal

6. Cyma reversa

3. Cavetto

7. Scotia

4. Ovolo

8. Torus

Mosaic. A surface decoration made of small marble or glass cubes called tesserae.

Necking. Also known as collarino, a wide molding at the top of a Tuscan, Doric, or Ionic column. *See* ORDERS OF architecture.

185

Orders of architecture (Five Orders). An order consists of a column with base (except in the Greek Doric), shaft, and capital and its entablature. Each order has its own formalized ornament. The orders are the basis of architectural design in the classical tradition, providing lessons in proportion, scale, and the uses of ornament. The five orders are Tuscan, Doric, Ionic Corinthian, and Composite. Although only the Ionic and the Corinthian are found in the Library of Congress, all five are shown here.

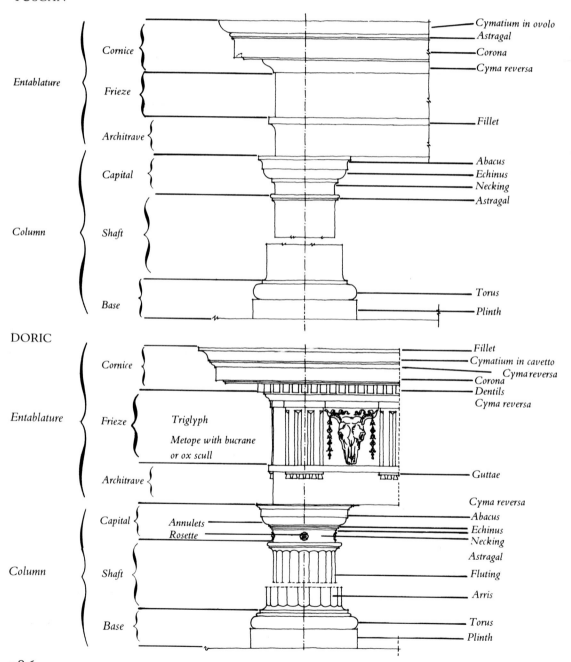

TUSCAN

Entablature
  Cornice — Cymatium in ovolo / Astragal / Corona / Cyma reversa
  Frieze
  Architrave — Fillet

Column
  Capital — Abacus / Echinus / Necking / Astragal
  Shaft
  Base — Torus / Plinth

DORIC

Entablature
  Cornice — Fillet / Cymatium in cavetto / Cyma reversa / Corona / Dentils / Cyma reversa
  Frieze — Triglyph / Metope with bucrane or ox scull
  Architrave — Guttae

Column
  Capital — Annulets / Rosette — Cyma reversa / Abacus / Echinus / Necking
  Shaft — Astragal / Fluting / Arris
  Base — Torus / Plinth

IONIC

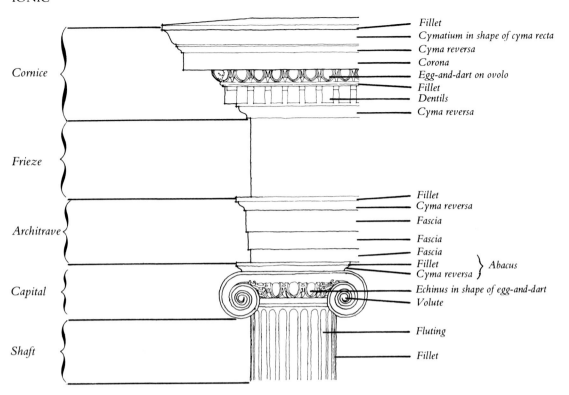

Cornice

Fillet
Cymatium in shape of cyma recta
Cyma reversa
Corona
Egg-and-dart on ovolo
Fillet
Dentils
Cyma reversa

Frieze

Architrave

Fillet
Cyma reversa
Fascia
Fascia
Fascia
Fillet
Cyma reversa } Abacus

Capital

Echinus in shape of egg-and-dart
Volute

Shaft

Fluting

Fillet

CORINTHIAN

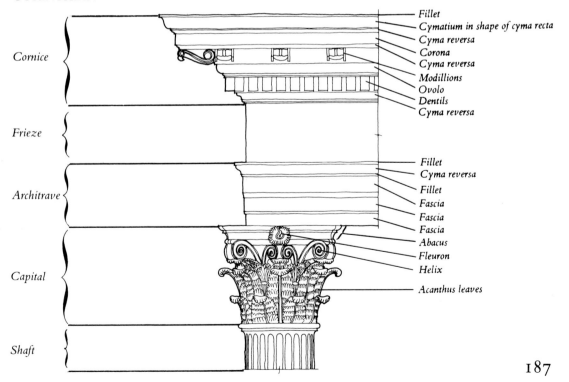

Cornice

Fillet
Cymatium in shape of cyma recta
Cyma reversa
Corona
Cyma reversa
Modillions
Ovolo
Dentils
Cyma reversa

Frieze

Architrave

Fillet
Cyma reversa
Fillet
Fascia
Fascia
Fascia
Abacus
Fleuron
Helix

Capital

Acanthus leaves

Shaft

187

COMPOSITE

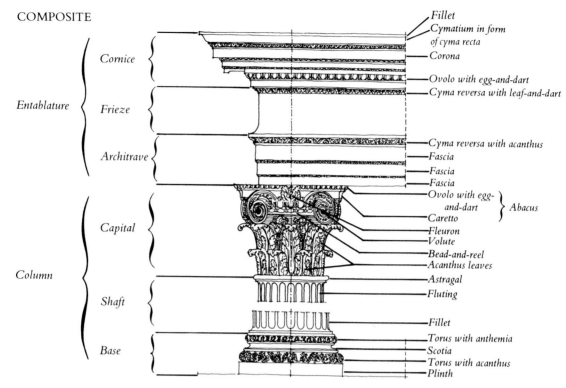

Entablature
- Cornice
- Frieze
- Architrave

Column
- Capital
- Shaft
- Base

Fillet
Cymatium in form of cyma recta
Corona
Ovolo with egg-and-dart
Cyma reversa with leaf-and-dart
Cyma reversa with acanthus
Fascia
Fascia
Fascia
Ovolo with egg-and-dart } Abacus
Caretto
Fleuron
Volute
Bead-and-reel
Acanthus leaves
Astragal
Fluting
Fillet
Torus with anthemia
Scotia
Torus with acanthus
Plinth

Ovolo. A convex molding, either ellipical or quarter-round. *See* MOLDINGS.

Pearls

Pearls. A small molding resembling a string of pearls. Also known as *Beads*.

Pedestal. The base for a column or a statue.

Pendentive. The triangular curving surface between two arches and beneath a dome.

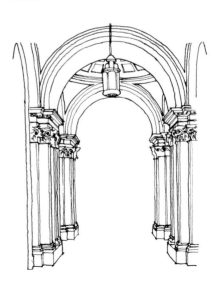

Pendentive

Pilaster. A vertical rectangular projection from the wall or a pier treated like a column by base, shaft, and capital.

Ribbon

Post. An upright supporting element.

Ribbon. An ornament in imitation of a cloth ribbon.

Rinceau (rinceaux, pl.). A symmetrical swirling of ornament of leaves, customarily those of the acanthus.

Rinceaux

Rosette. A floral motive, round or square, customarily found in coffers.

Saucer dome. A low concave ceiling, taking the shape of an inverted saucer.

Rosette

Scroll. A spiral found in the form of volutes of a capital or in the frame of a cartouche.

Scroll frame. A frame adorned with scrolls.

Scroll Frames

Shaft. The trunk or the longest part of a column between the base and the capital. *See* ORDERS OF ARCHITECTURE.

Soffit. The underside of an arch, a beam, or any spanning member.

Spandrel. The triangular space bounded by the curve of an arch, a horizontal line through its top, and a vertical line rising from the impost or springing of the arch.

Swag. *See* FESTOON.

Triglyph. A projecting block with three channels forming part of a Doric frieze. *See* ORDERS OF ARCHITECTURE, DORIC.

Tripod. A three-legged utensil; among the Greeks and Romans, a three-legged vessel used for sacrifices.

Vault. An arched ceiling.

Volute. A spiral scroll as on an Ionic or Corinthian capital, or any spiral ornament. *See* ORDERS OF ARCHITECTURE.

APPENDIX II:
Biographical Dictionary of the Artists, Architects, and One Engineer of the Library of Congress with a Brief Biography of Herbert Small

For assistance in gathering information, the editor wishes to thank John Dobkin, director of the National Academy of Design, and two members of his staff, Cassandra Denny and Barbara Krulik, Lawrence Campbell, editor of *Art Students League News,* Faith Hommel Vosburgh, assistant librarian of the American Institute of Architects, Florian H. Thayn of the Office of the Architect of the Capitol, Mrs. Alexander Buel Trowbridge, Theodora Morgan, managing editor, *National Sculpture Review,* and Helen Johnson. —HHR

HERBERT SMALL, journalist and publisher, was born in Milwaukee, Wisconsin, in 1869. Evidently, his family moved to Boston, for we find him attending the Boston Latin School and, later, Harvard College, class of 1891. He did not graduate, leaving college in his senior year to take up journalism. While working for the *Boston Herald* he wrote a guide to the Boston Public Library. Book publishing next drew him. He organized Small, Maynard & Company, which had, among its titles, the first two "Mr. Dooley" books of Finley Peter Dunne. The firm lasted only three years.

Somehow he found time to write this splendid guide, originally entitled *Handbook of the New Library of Congress in Washington,* published in Boston in 1897. He did not assume full credit, noting on the title page that it had been "compiled by Herbert Small." In addition, there were essays on the architecture, sculpture, and painting by the artist-writer Charles H. Caffin, and the function of a national library by the librarian Ainsworth R. Spofford as well as a preface by Small himself. These were dropped in the 1901 edition, which is the text of the book in hand. "Compiled by" was retained in the 1901 edition; but with the book having a new title, Herbert Small has now been given full credit as author.

He left this note of explanation and acknowledgment at the close of his preface to the 1897 edition: "The writer desires to express his great obligation, for much information and courtesy, to Mr. Bernard R. Green [the engineer] in charge of the Library during the time that this book was preparing, to Mr. Edward Pearce Casey [the architect] and to Mr. Spofford [librarian when the building was under construction]; without their assistance the book could hardly have been written. Thanks are due, also to many of the individual artists for their courtesy in explaining the meaning and application of their work—and in particular to Mr. Elmer E. Garnsey [the artist in charge of the decoration] for a great deal of painstaking assistance."

That is the sum of information we have on this book.

Small, after giving up publishing, founded the Publicity Bureau of Boston and also became secretary of the Germanic Museum Association of Harvard. By this time he was married and had two children. He died of typhoid in the city hospital in 1903.

NA—National Academician or Member, National Academy of Design.
ANA—Associate, National Academy, or Associate Member, National Academy of Design.

HERBERT ADAMS, NA, sculptor, 1858–1945. Born in West Concord, Vermont. Studied sculpture in Boston, then in Paris under Antonin Mercié from 1885 to 1890. Influenced by Saint-Gaudens. Did bronze doors of Saint Bartholomew's Church, Hoyt Memorial in Judson Memorial Church, statue of William Cullen Bryant in Bryant Park, all in New York. Statues on Brooklyn Museum and Pratt Memorial Angel in Baptist Emmanuel Church, both in Brooklyn. William Ellery Channing statue in Boston, Massachusetts; Jonathan Edwards Memorial in Northampton, Massachusetts; statue of Chief Justice Marshall in Cleveland, Ohio; and McMillan Fountain in Washington. President, National Academy of Design, 1917–1920.

JOHN WHITE ALEXANDER NA, painter, 1856–1915. Born in Allegheny, Pennsylvania. At eighteen began illustrating for *Harper's Weekly*. In Paris in 1877, then Munich at the Royal Academy, where he met Frank Duveneck and Walter Shirlaw. Later in Italy, where he came to know Whistler and Henry James. In New York in 1881 making his reputation as a leading portrait painter. Returned to Europe on and off, not settling in New York until 1901. Instructor at Art Students League of New York, 1902–1903. In 1905 commissioned to paint forty-eight panels for Carnegie Institute in Pittsburgh for $175,000. President, National Academy of Design, 1909–1915.

GEORGE RANDOLPH BARSE, JR., NA, painter, 1861–1938. Born in Detroit. From 1878 to 1884 studying under Cabanel, Boulanger, and Lefebvre. Instructor at Art Students League, 1894–1896. Noted for figures and portraits.

PAUL WAYLAND BARTLETT, NA, sculptor, 1865–1925. Born in New Haven, Connecticut. Went to Paris in 1870s to study under Frémiet and Carriès. Did animal groups to be found in Jardin des Plantes, Paris. Did *Bear Tamer* in the Corcoran Gallery, Washington, General Washington in Philadelphia, General McClellan in Philadelphia, General Warren in Boston, and General Lafayette in Paris, all equestrian. Benjamin Franklin in Waterbury, Connecticut. Six statues on attic of New York Public Library, assisted J. Q. A. Ward with sculpture in pediment of New York Stock Exchange, and did pediment of House Wing of United States Capitol.

THEODORE BAUR, sculptor, 1835–?. Born in Württemberg. Came to America in 1850. Worked on Parliament Houses in Ottawa.

FRANK WESTON BENSON, NA, painter, 1862–1951. Born in Salem, Massachusetts. Went to Boston Museum of Fine Arts School. In Paris studied under Boulanger and Lefebvre. Taught in Portland, Maine, and at Boston Museum School. Impressionist. Member of "The Ten," a group of Boston and New York artists of whom best known was Childe Hassam. Most famous as etcher of waterfowl.

GEORGE EDWIN BISSELL, sculptor, 1839–1920. Born in New Preston, Connecticut. Began as stone carver and in marble business in Poughkeepsie. Career began in 1870, in 1875–1876 in Paris, Florence, and Rome, and again from 1883–1886 in Paris. Did Soldiers Memorial in Waterbury, Connecticut; President Chester A. Arthur in Philadelphia; Lincoln in Edinburgh, Scotland; Chancellor John Watts in Trinity Churchyard, and Mayor Abraham de Peyster, both in New York.

EDWIN HOWLAND BLASHFIELD, NA, painter, 1848–1936. Born in Brooklyn, went to Massachusetts Institute of Technology for two years. In 1867 went to Paris on advice of William Morris Hunt. Studied under Léon Bonnat from 1867 to 1870 and from 1874 to 1880. Instructor at Art Students League of New York, 1888–1890. His first mural decoration executed at World's Columbian Exposition of 1893, Chicago. Most successful mural decorator of period 1890–1930. Work in Curtis School of Music (formerly George W. C. Drexel residence), Philadelphia; Baltimore Courthouse; Minnesota State Capitol in St. Paul; Iowa State Capitol in Des Moines; Appellate Court in Madison Square, New York; Great Hall at College of the City of New York, City University of New York; Mahoning County Courthouse in Youngstown, Ohio; Hudson County Courthouse in Jersey City; Luzerne County Courthouse in Wilkes-Barre, Pennsylvania; United States Courthouse in Cleveland, Ohio; Wisconsin State Capitol in Madison; Detroit Public Library;

Cathedral of Saint Matthew the Apostle in Washington; Elks National Memorial in Chicago; and Walker Memorial in Massachusetts Institute of Technology, Cambridge. President, National Academy of Design, 1920–1926.

JOHN JOSEPH BOYLE, ANA, sculptor, 1851–1917. Born in New York. Began as stone carver. Studied at Pennsylvania Academy of Fine Arts and in Paris. Did *The Indian Family* in Lincoln Park, Chicago; *The Stone Age,* Fairmount Park, Philadelphia; and *Benjamin Franklin* in Philadelphia, with replica of same in Paris.

CHARLES H. CAFFIN, writer, 1854–1918. Born in Sittingbourne, Kent, England. Went to Magdalen College, Oxford. Came to U.S.A. in 1892 and did decorative work at World's Columbian Exposition of 1893, Chicago. Art critic for *Harper's Weekly, Evening Post* (New York), *Sun* (New York), *New York American,* and *Studio.* Wrote *Photography as a Fine Art, American Masters of Painting, American Masters of Sculpture, The Story of American Painting,* among others.

EDWARD PEARCE CASEY, architect, 1864–1940. Born in Portland, Maine, son of General Thomas Lincoln Casey. Degree in civil engineering, Columbia School of Mines, New York, in Atelier Laloux of École des Beaux Arts. Went to New York in 1891 where he practiced architecture. Designed Connecticut Avenue Bridge, Grant Monument with sculptor Henry Mervin Shrady at foot of National Capitol, and Continental Memorial Hall for the Daughters of the American Revolution, all in Washington.

THOMAS LINCOLN CASEY, soldier, 1831–1896. Born in Sackett's Harbor, New York. West Point, 1852. Later assistant professor of Engineering at West Point. In 1859–1861, commanded U.S. Engineers on West Coast, then occupied with fortress construction in Northeast. Superintendent of Public Buildings in Washington when present Executive Office (formerly State, War and Navy) Building, Washington Aqueduct, and Washington Monument under construction. In 1888, brigadier general, chief of U.S. Engineers.

KENYON COX, NA, painter, 1856–1919. Born in Warren, Ohio. Went to art school in Cincinnati, in 1876 at Pennsylvania Academy of Art, Philadelphia, in 1877 in ateliers of Carolus Duran, Cabanel, and Gérôme in Paris. From 1883 on in New York. Instructor Art Students League, 1885–1909. Did murals at World's Columbian Exposition of 1893, Chicago. Mural work to be found in Walker Art Gallery, Bowdoin College, Maine; Appellate Court in Madison Square, New York; Hudson County Courthouse, Jersey City; Essex County Courthouse, Newark, New Jersey; Luzerne County Courthouse in Wilkes-Barre, Pennsylvania; Federal Building, Cleveland, Ohio; Oberlin College, Oberlin, Ohio; Iowa State Capitol in Des Moines; Wisconsin State Capitol in Madison; Minnesota State Capitol in St. Paul; and Public Library, Winona, Wisconsin. Author of *The Classic Point of View,* best book on painting by an American, now part of Classical America Series in Art and Architecture, and of other essays on art.

PAUL PHILIPPE CRET, architect, NA, 1876–1945. Born in Lyons, France. Went to École des Beaux Arts, Lyons, then in Atelier Pascal, École des Beaux Arts, Paris. In 1903 taught at School of Architecture, University of Pennsylvania, where he remained until 1937. Among works: Pan American Union, Folger Shakespeare Library, and Federal Reserve Board Building, all in Washington; Washington Memorial Arch, Valley Forge; Benjamin Franklin Bridge, Rodin Museum, and Federal Reserve Bank, all in Philadelphia; Indianapolis Public Library, Detroit Institute of Fine Arts, development plan and buildings for University of Texas, Austin; San Antonio Post Office; Barnes Foundation Gallery, Merion, Pennsylvania; buildings for United States Military Academy, West Point. Towards the end of his career, Cret abandoned the classical and he made a considerable contribution towards the design of the streamlined express train of the nineteen thirties.

ROBERT M. CRONBACH, sculptor, b. 1908. Born in St. Louis. Attended St. Louis School of Fine Arts and Pennsylvania Academy of Art. Worked in Federal Arts Project in 1930s. Work in Social Security Building in Washington, D.C.; St. Louis Municipal Auditorium and fountain in Federal Building, St. Louis; also in United Nations General Assembly Building.

CYRUS EDWIN DALLIN, NA, sculptor, 1861–1944. Born in Springville, Utah. Lived with Indians. Studied under Truman Bartlett in Boston. In 1888 to Paris at École des Beaux Arts and Académie Julien. Worked in Boston. Equestrian statues: *The Signal of Peace* in Lincoln Park, Chicago; *The Medicine Man* in Fairmount Park, Philadelphia; and *The Appeal of the Great Spirit,* Boston. He also did statue of Paul Revere in Boston.

ROSCOE PLIMPTON DEWITT, architect, 1894–1975. Born in Dallas, Texas. Went to Dartmouth College and Harvard School of Architecture. Partner in DeWitt & Lemmon, DeWitt & Washburn, DeWitt & Swanke and Office of Roscoe DWitt, all in Dallas. Associate architect on the extension of the East Front of National Capitol, architect of Library, Stadium and Administration Building of Southern Methodist University, Dallas.

FREDERICK DIELMAN, NA, painter, 1847–1935. Born in Hanover, Germany. Brought as child to Baltimore. From 1866 to 1872, topographer and draftsman with United States Engineers. Studied under Wilhelm Diez at Royal Academy in Munich from 1872 to 1876. In 1876 had studio in New York. Taught at Art Students League of New York, 1878–1886, 1897–1898, 1899–1903. Did mosaic panels for Albany Savings Bank in Albany, New York; six mosaic panels for Pennsylvania State Capitol in Harrisburg; six mosaic panels for Iowa State Capitol in Des Moines. From 1903 to 1918, professor of drawing at College of the City of New York, and from 1903 to 1931 director of Art School of Cooper Union. President of National Academy of Design from 1900 to 1909.

ROBERT LEFTWICH DODGE, painter, 1872–1940. Born in Bedford, Virginia. Did stained glass for churches in New York, Minneapolis, and Baltimore and for the Vassar Chapel, Poughkeepsie.

WILLIAM DE LEFTWICH DODGE, painter, 1867–1935. Born in Bedford, Virginia. Studied in Munich and Paris, in latter city under Léon Gérôme. Illustrator for *Le Figaro Illustré, Collier's Magazine,* and other publications. Worked at World's Columbian Exposition of 1893, Chicago. Murals to be found in Brooklyn Academy of Music; New York State Capitol in Albany; City Hall of Buffalo; New York courthouse in Syracuse, New York; Teachers College in Cedar Falls, Iowa. Taught at Art Students League of New York 1915–1916, 1925–1929.

JOHN DONOGHUE, sculptor, 1853–1903. Born in Chicago. Went to Chicago Academy of Design. Studied under Jouffroy and Falguière in Paris, also in Rome.

FRANK ELISCU, NA, sculptor, b. 1912. Born in Brooklyn. Went to Bronx Institute of Design and Pratt Institute. Taught sculpture at School of Industrial Arts in New York. Did *Atoms for Peace* in Ventura, California. Executed inaugural medal for President Ford.

HENRY JACKSON ELLICOTT, sculptor, 1848–1901. Born near Ellicott City, Maryland. Studied at National Academy of Design, New York. Equestrian statues of General Hancock, Washington, and General McClellan in Philadelphia. Statues for the city and state of New York at Gettysburg, and statue of Duncan Monument in Pittsburgh.

JOHN FLANAGAN, NA, sculptor, 1865–1952. Born in Newark, New Jersey. Attended Cooper Union, New York. Worked for Ellin & Kitson in Perth Amboy Terra Cotta Works. Studied under Saint-Gaudens in New York and Chapu and Falguière in Paris.

Bronze relief for Newark, New Jersey, Public Library and Langley Memorial in Smithsonian Institution.

DANIEL CHESTER FRENCH, NA, sculptor, 1850–1931. Born in Exeter, New Hampshire. Studied under J. Q. A. Ward in New York, Thomas Ball in Boston, and Preston Powers in Florence. Did famous *Minute Man* in Concord in 1875, and in 1882 *John Harvard* on Harvard campus, Cambridge, Massachusetts. In Paris in 1886–1887, permanently in New York after 1887. Instructor, Art Students League of New York, 1890–1891, 1898–1899. Statue of the Republic in Jackson Park, Chicago; smaller version of same done for World's Columbian Exposition of 1893, Chicago. Also quadriga on Minnesota State Capitol in St. Paul; equestrian General Grant in Fairmount Park, Philadelphia; equestrian Washington in Paris; equestrian General Hooker in Boston; relief of Lafayette in Prospect Park in Brooklyn; statue groups of Four Continents at Bowling Green, New York; bronze doors of Boston Public Library; seated Lincoln in Lincoln Memorial, Washington.

ELMER ELLSWORTH GARNSEY, painter, 1862–1946. Born in Holmdel, Monmouth County, New Jersey. Attended Cooper Union and Art Students League in New York. Studied with George Maynard and Francis Lathrop. In 1882–1889, assistant to both Lathrop and then Maynard. In 1892, aide to Francis D. Millet at World's Columbian Exposition in Chicago. Did color decoration of Boston Public Library and Carnegie Institute in Pittsburgh; also St. Louis Public Library; Low Library, Columbia University, New York; Memorial Hall, Yale University, New Haven, Connecticut; Minnesota State Capitol at St. Paul; Iowa State Capitol at Des Moines; Wisconsin State Capitol at Madison. Did color scheme for Manufacturers Hanover Bank Branch on Montague Street, Brooklyn. Did series of city views for office in United States Custom House on Bowling Green, New York, and panels for the library of the Andrew Carnegie residence, now Cooper-Hewitt Museum, in New York.

BERNARD RICHARDSON GREEN, engineer and inventor, 1843–1914. Born in Malden, Massachusetts. Graduate of Lawrence Scientific School, Harvard, 1863. In charge of fortress construction for federal government. Supervised construction of State, War and Navy Building, now Executive Office Building. Did much of engineering on Washington Monument. Devised system of book stacks for Library of Congress. In charge of construction of Army Medical Museum and consultant in construction of New York Public Library.

CARL GUTHERZ, painter, 1844–1907. Born in Aargau, Switzerland. In 1851 moved with family to Cincinnati and a year later to Memphis. Worked with father, a terra-cotta sculptor. Studied under Cabason, Pils, Bouguereau, and Lefebvre in Paris, Stallaert and Robert in Brussels and Antwerp, and Simonetti in Rome. Also in Munich. Back in Memphis in 1873. Founded Art Department of Washington University, St. Louis. Decorated People's Church, St. Paul, Minnesota.

WALKER HANCOCK, NA, sculptor, b. 1901. Born in St. Louis, Missouri. Went to Washington University, St. Louis School of Fine Arts, and Pennsylvania Academy of Fine Arts. Rome Fellow, 1928, at American Academy in Rome. Did statue of John Paul Jones in Fairmount Park, Philadelphia; worked on Stone Mountain Memorial in Georgia; did bust of Stephen Foster for Hall of Fame in New York. Designed Distinguished Flying Cross decoration and Eisenhower-Nixon Inaugural Medal, 1952.

JONATHAN SCOTT HARTLEY, NA, sculptor, sculptor, 1845–1912. Born in Albany, New York. Studied with Erastus Dow Palmer and Lemuel E. Wilmarth at Art Students League of New York. Spent three years at Royal Academy, London, then in Berlin, Rome, and Paris. In 1875 had studio in New York. Did John Ericsson Monument in Battery Park, New York; Miles Morgan statue in Springfield, Massachusetts; Alfred the Great on Appellate Court in Madison Square, New York; Reverend Thomas E. Beecher in Elmira, New York; and Daguerre Monument in Washington.

EDWARD J. HOLSLAG, painter, 1870–1925. Born in Buffalo, New York. Studied under John La Farge. Lived in Chicago. Active in decorating hotels.

WALTER MCEWEN, ANA, painter, 1860–1943. Born in Chicago. At Royal Academy in Munich with Frank Duveneck, Currier, Neal, and other American artists. Then in Holland. Studied under Cormon and Robert-Fleury in Paris. Lived in Paris. Best known as genre and portrait painter.

WILLIAM ANDREW MACKAY, painter, 1878–1934. Born in Philadelphia. Studied under Robert Reid in New York and Constant and Laurens in Paris. Has work in Minnesota State Capitol in St. Paul; Essex County Courthouse in Newark, New Jersey; and large murals in Theodore Roosevelt Memorial, American Museum of Natural History, New York.

FREDERICK WILLIAM MACMONNIES, NA, sculptor, 1863–1937. Born in Brooklyn. Drew and modeled from boyhood. At sixteen in studio of Augustus Saint-Gaudens where he did modeling, casting in plaster, marble cutting, and bronze casting. Studied at night at National Academy of Design and Art Students League. At twenty in Paris in the Falguière atelier of the École des Beaux Arts. At twenty-three won Prix d'Atelier, highest prize open to foreigners. Did statues of J. S. T. Stranahan in Prospect Park and Nathan Hale in City Hall Park in New York. Chosen by Saint-Gaudens to do *Ship of State,* with twenty-seven figures, most important sculptural work at World's Columbian Exposition of 1893 in Chicago. Did four spandrel figures for Washington Arch (1894) in Washington Square, New York; *Victory* (1895) for West Point Battle Monument; groups (1895–1900) for Soldiers and Sailors Monument in Brooklyn's Grand Army Plaza. Turned briefly to painting. Then followed Pioneer Monument (1905) in Denver, General George B. McLellan equestrian (1906) in Washington, *Inspiration and Truth* (1913) to either side of main entrance of New York Public Library, Civic Virtue (1919) at Queens Borough Hall, New York, Princeton Battle Monument (1922), and American Monument, Battle of the Marne, Meaux, France (1926).

PHILIP MARTINY, ANA, sculptor, 1858–1927. Born in Strasbourg, France. Studied under Eugene Dock. Came to New York as young man. Assisted Saint-Gaudens on mantelpiece for Cornelius Vanderbilt mansion, now in American Wing, Metropolitan Museum of Art, also on latter's statue of Puritan. Worked on McKim, Mead & White's Agricultural Building at World's Columbian Exposition, 1893. Sculpture to be found at Hall of Records of New York City, and on Soldiers and Sailors Monument, Grand Army Plaza, Brooklyn. Did lions in Boston Public Library; *Doughboy* in Abingdon Square, Greenwich Village, New York; bronze doors of Saint Bartholomew's Church, also in New York; Soldiers and Sailors Monument in Jersey City; and statue of Vice-President Hobart in Paterson, N.J.

GEORGE WILLOUGHBY MAYNARD, NA, painter, 1843–1923. Born in Washington, D.C. Studied at National Academy of Design and Art Students League of New York, also under E. White in Florence, and in Rome and at Royal Academy in Antwerp. Did work in St. John's Church, Jamaica Plain, Massachusetts; Essex County Courthouse in Newark, New Jersey; Appellate Court in Madison Square, New York; and ceiling of auditorium of old Metropolitan Opera House in New York. Also did bronze inlay of floor of vestibule in Low Library, Columbia University, New York.

GARI MELCHERS, NA, painter, 1860–1932. Born in Detroit. Studied in Düsseldorf, then in Paris under Boulanger and Lefebvre. Lived most of time in Paris and Holland. Worked at World's Columbian Exposition of 1893, Chicago. From 1909 to 1914 in Weimar, Germany. Did mural work in Detroit Public Library.

CHARLES HENRY NIEHAUS, NA, sculptor, 1855–1935. Born in Cincinnati, Ohio. In 1877–1880 in Royal Academy in Munich. In 1881 back in Cincinnati. Did statues of President Garfield and William Allen in Cincinnati. To New York in 1887. Did pediments of Appellate Court, Madison Square, New York; Kentucky State Capitol in Frankfort; seated Lincoln in Chicago; doors of Trinity Church, New York; John Paul Jones and Hahnemann Monument in Washington; Francis Scott Key Memorial in Baltimore; equestrian General N. B. Forrest in Memphis; McKinley Tomb in Canton, Ohio; and St. Louis of France in St. Louis.

CHARLES SPRAGUE PEARCE, ANA, painter, 1851–1914. Born in Boston. Studied under Léon Bonnat in Paris. Did work for *Paris Illustré*. Lived at Auvers-sur-Oise most of his life, painting in France and Algeria.

PAUL J. PELZ, architect, 1841–1918. Born in Silesia, Germany. Came to U.S.A. in 1851. In 1859–1866 in office of Detlef Lienau in New York. Architect for U.S. Lighthouse Board. In 1873 with John L. Smithmeyer entered competition for Library of Congress design and won first prize of $1,500. In 1886 named assistant architect of Library and in 1888 architect. Superseded in 1892 by Edward Pearce Casey. With Smithmeyer did U.S. Army and Navy Hospital in Hot Springs, Arkansas; Academic Building at Georgetown University, Washington, D.C.; Carnegie Library and Music Hall in Alleghany, Pennsylvania. On his own did private residences in Washington.

ROLAND HINTON PERRY, sculptor and painter, 1870–1941. Born in New York. In Paris from 1890 to 1894, where he studied under Gérôme, Delance, Callot, Chapu, and Puech. In New York in 1894. Did lions for Connecticut Avenue Bridge, Washington; equestrian General John B. Castleman, Louisville, Kentucky; statues of General George S. Greene and General Wadsworth at Gettyburg, General Curtis in Ogdensburg, New York; reliefs in New Amsterdam Theater (Florenz Ziegfeld's theater) at Times Square, New York; and statues on dome of Pennsylvania State Capitol in Harrisburg.

CHARLES ADAMS PLATT, NA, landscape architect, architect, 1861–1933. Born in New York. Went to school of National Academy of Design. Studied etching under Stephen Parrish, father of Maxfield Parrish. Etched views of harbors along Northeast Coast. In 1882–1887 mostly in Europe, etching and painting. In 1890 turned to garden design in Cornish, New Hampshire. In 1892 trip to Italy to study gardens. *Italian Gardens,* 1894. In 1900 turned to architecture. Did houses in Cornish, New Hampshire, South Manchester, Connecticut; Cleveland, Ohio; twin houses for Mrs. James Roosevelt and Franklin Delano Roosevelt in New York; house and garden for Mrs. Harold F. McCormick in Lake Forest, Illinois; McMillan Memorial Fountain and Freer Gallery in Washington; house for Eugene Meyer, Jr. in Mount Kisco, New York; buildings for Connecticut College for Women in New London; buildings at Phillips Academy, Exeter, Massachusetts; and apartment houses for Vincent Astor Estate in New York.

ALFRED EASTON POOR, NA, architect, b. 1899. Born in Baltimore. Studied at Harvard and at School of Architecture, University of Pennsylvania. Did Parke-Bernet Gallery, Queens County Courthouse, United States Custom House and Federal Office, and McGraw-Hill Building, all in New York City. One of several architects who executed extension of East Front of the National Capitol. President, National Academy of Design, 1966–1977.

CANDIDO PORTINARI, painter, 1903–1962. Born in Brodowski, near São Paulo, Brazil. Went to School of Fine Arts in Rio. In 1928–1930 in Europe where he turned antiacademic. Murals in Ministry of Education in Rio de Janeiro, at College of Cataguanzes, and in numerous Brazilian churches. Also did murals in United Nations Building, New York.

EDWARD CLARK POTTER, NA, sculptor, 1857–1923. Born in New London, Connecticut. Studied under Mercié and Frémiet in Paris, later in studio of Daniel Chester French. Equestrian statues of General Grant, Philadelphia; General Washington, Paris; General Hooker, Boston; and General Slocum, Gettysburg. Did famous lions in front of New York Public Library. Also did all of animals in statues by Daniel Chester French.

BELA LYON PRATT, ANA, sculptor, 1867–1917. Born in Norwich, Connecticut. Studied with Saint-Gaudens, William Merritt Chase, and Kenyon Cox in New York and Falguière in Paris. Did Nathan Hale at Yale University, New Haven, Connecticut; Edward Everett Hale in Boston Public Gardens; sculpture on façade of Boston Museum of Fine Arts.

ROBERT REID, NA, painter, 1862–1929. Born in Stockbridge, Massachusetts. Studied at Boston Museum of Fine Arts School and Art Students League of New York. In ateliers of Boulanger and Lefebvre in Paris. One of eight mural painters at work in Manufacturers and Liberal Arts Building of World's Columbian Exposition of 1893, Chicago. Mural work in Appellate Court, New York, and Massachusetts State House, Boston. Did window for Church of Saint Paul the Apostle, New York. Part of group of New York and Boston Impressionists called "The Ten," the best known of whom was Childe Hassam.

FREDERICK WELLINGTON RUCKSTULL, sculptor, 1853–1942. Born in Breitenbach, Alsace. Brought to St. Louis as child. Studied in St. Louis and later in Paris under Boulanger, Lefebvre, and Mercié. After 1892 established in New York. Seated statues in front of Appellate Court, New York; statue of Minerva, Green-Wood Cemetery, Brooklyn; Confederate Monument in Baltimore; equestrian statues of General Hartranft in Harrisburg, Pennsylvania, and General Wade Hampton in Columbia, South Carolina; and statues of John C. Calhoun, Uriah M. Rose, and Wade Hampton in Statuary Hall of the National Capitol. Best remembered for his fight against modern art.

AUGUSTUS SAINT-GAUDENS, NA, sculptor, 1848–1907. Born in Dublin, Ireland. Brought to New York in 1848. Studied at Cooper Union and National Academy of Design in New York. Was cameo cutter. In 1867 in Paris studying with Jouffroy; in 1870 in Rome. Instructor at Art Students League of New York 1887–1890 and 1891–1898. Did Captain Randall, Sailors Snug Harbor, Staten Island, Admiral Farragut in Madison Square, Peter Cooper at Cooper Union, equestrian General William Tecumseh Sherman in Manhattan's Grand Army Plaza, all in New York; Parnell in O'Connell Street, Dublin, Ireland; Lincoln and equestrian General Logan in Chicago; Phillips Brooks at Trinity Church and Shaw Memorial across from Massachusetts State House both in Boston; eight caryatides for Albright Art Gallery, Buffalo, New York; and Adams Memorial in Rock Creek Cemetery, Washington.

LOUIS SAINT-GAUDENS, sculptor, 1854–1913. Born in New York, the younger brother of Augustus Saint-Gaudens. Like him began as cameo cutter. In 1878 joined brother in Paris and helped him with casting of Admiral Farragut now in New York. Also worked with brother on chimneypiece for Cornelius Vanderbilt mansion now in Metropolitan Museum of Art. Did six statues for Union Station in Washington; two statues for United States Custom House on Bowling Green, New York; relief for Church of the Ascension and baptismal font of Church of the Incarnation, both in New York.

HERMAN T. SCHLADERMUNDT, painter, 1863–1937. Born in Milwaukee, Wisconsin. Worked for Burnham & Root in Chicago. Attended Académie Julien and Académie Delacluse in Paris for a year. Worked on decoration of Hotel Ponce de Leon, Saint Augustine, Florida, for Carrère & Hastings. Worked with George W. Maynard in decorating McKim, Mead & White's Agricultural Building at World's Columbian Exposition of 1893, Chicago. Did glass for Emigrant Industrial Savings Bank on Chambers Street, Board of

Directors Room, old General Motors Building, both in New York; Central Congregational Church in Providence, Rhode Island, and Missouri State Capitol in Jefferson City.

JESSE M. SHELTON, architect, 1895–1976. Born in Atlanta and went to Georgia Institute of Technology. Officer of Robert and Company, later Robert and Company Associates, architects-engineers. Architect for Coca-Cola Company and for Bureau of Prisons, Department of Justice.

WALTER SHIRLAW, NA, painter, 1838–1909. Born in Paisley, Scotland. Brought to New York at three, later in Chicago. Began as engraver; turned to painting. From 1870 to 1877 in Munich studying under Wagner, Raab, Ramberg and Lindenschmidt. Instructor at Art Students League of New York 1877–1878, 1879–1881, 1883–1889, 1890–1891. Did genre and portraits besides mural work.

EDWARD SIMMONS, painter, 1852–1931. Born in Concord, Massachusetts. Went to Harvard, class of 1874. A founder of the *Harvard Crimson.* Oil salesman in Cincinnati, store clerk in San Francisco, teacher. At Boston Museum of Fine Arts School 1877–1878; then to Paris, where he studied with Lefebvre and Boulanger. From 1891 worked in New York. Instructor at Art Students League of New York. At World's Columbian Exposition of 1893, Chicago. Mural decoration in Minnesota State Capitol in St. Paul; South Dakota State Capitol in Bismarck; Massachusetts State House in Boston; courthouses in Des Moines, Iowa, and in Mercer, Pennsylvania; Appellate Court in Madison Square, New York; and John D. Rockefeller residence in Pocantico Hills, New York, and Frederick Vanderbilt mansion at Hyde Park, New York.

JOHN L. SMITHMEYER, architect, 1832–1908. Born in Vienna. Came to U.S.A. in 1848. In Chicago and Indianapolis. Superintendent of Public Buildings in the South in the Office of United States Supervising Architect after the Civil War. Became partner of Paul J. Pelz in 1872 and won competition for Library of Congress in 1873. Named architect in 1886, dismissed in 1888. With Pelz did U.S. Army and Navy Hospital in Hot Springs, Arkansas; Academic Building at Georgetown University, Washington, D.C.; Carnegie Library Music Hall in Alleghany, Pennsylvania.

W. MILLS THOMPSON, painter, 1875–1934. Born in Washington. Attended Corcoran Art School in Washington and Art Students League in New York. Art editor, *Saturday Evening Post.*

FRANÇOIS M. L. TONETTI-DOZZI, sculptor, 1863–1920. Born in Paris, studied under Tony-Noël and Falguière. Worked with Frederick Mac-

Monnies on Columbian Fountain for World's Columbian Exposition of 1893, Chicago, and on groups for Soldiers and Sailors Monument, Grand Army Plaza, Brooklyn. Did statues of Venice and Spain on old Custom House, Bowling Green, New York; mantel of Directors' Room in New York Public Library; sculpture for Connecticut State Library in Hartford, and for garden of John D. Rockefeller in Pocantico Hills, New York.

ALEXANDER BUEL TROWBRIDGE, architect, 1868–1950. Born in Detroit, Michigan. Cornell University, 1890, in Atelier Marcel Lambert, École des Beaux Arts, 1893–1895. Dean of School of Architecture, Cornell, 1897–1902. From 1906 to 1921 partner in Trowbridge & Ackerman; executed Central Branch, YMCA, Brooklyn, 1914. Consulting architect to Federal Reserve Bank of New York, 1918–1924; to Federal Reserve Board, Washington, D.C., 1919; Hampton Institute; Folger Shakespeare Memorial Library, where he was also associate architect; and George Washington University, Washington, D.C.

WILLIAM BRANTLEY VAN INGEN, painter, 1858–1955. Born in Philadelphia. Studied under Christian Schuessele and Thomas Eakins in Philadelphia, under John La Farge, Francis Lathrop, and Louis Comfort Tiffany in New York, and Léon Bonnat in Paris. Decorated U.S. Mint, Philadelphia; Pennsylvania State Capitol, Harrisburg; New Jersey State Capitol, Trenton; Administration Building, Panama Canal Zone; and U.S. Courthouse and Post Office in Indianapolis; New York State College for Teachers, Albany.

ELIHU VEDDER, NA, painter, 1836–1923. Born in New York. In 1856 in Paris studying under Picot. Later in Düsseldorf, Florence, and Rome. Had studio in New York in 1861 when at work on illustrations. From 1867 on in Rome and remained there till his death with occasional returns to United States. In 1886 illustrated famous edition of *Rubáiyát of Omar Khayyam*. Mural work in Walker Art Gallery, Bowdoin College, Maine; and in Collis P. Huntington's New York house, this last now in Yale University Art Gallery.

HENRY OLIVER WALKER, NA, painter, 1843–1929. Born in Boston. Studied under Léon Bonnat in Paris. Returned to Boston and then moved to New York. His mural work is to be found in Massachusetts State House in Boston, Appellate Court on Madison Square in New York, Minnesota State Capitol in St. Paul, and Essex County Courthouse in Newark, New Jersey.

JOHN QUINCY ADAMS WARD, NA, sculptor, 1830–1910. Born in Urbana, Ohio. Assistant to Henry Kirke Brown in New York. Did work on equestrian Washington in Union Square, executed Indian

Hunter, Seventh Regiment Memorial, Shakespeare and Pilgrim in Central Park, Horace Greeley in City Hall Park, Washington in Wall Street, and pediment of New York Stock Exchange all in New York; Henry Ward Beecher in Borough Hall Park in Brooklyn; Commodore Oliver Hazard Perry in Newport, Rhode Island; and equestrian General Thomas in Thomas Circle and President Garfield Memorial on Capitol Grounds in Washington. President, National Academy of Design, 1873–1874.

OLIN LEVI WARNER, NA, sculptor, 1844–1896. Born in Suffield, Connecticut. Made enough money as telegraph operator to go to Paris at twenty-five. Studied under Jouffroy and Carpeaux. Settled in New York, studied under Lemuel S. Wilmarth at Art Students League of New York. No commissions, so returned to family farm and worked for silver and bronze manufacturers and did portrait busts. Statue of Governor William A. Buckingham in Connecticut State Capitol in Hartford; terra-cotta busts on façade of Long Island Historical Society in Brooklyn; statue of William Lloyd Garrison on Commonwealth Avenue, Boston; and fountain in Portland, Oregon.

ALBERT WEINERT, sculptor, 1863–1947. Born in Leipzig and attended Royal Academy in Leipzig. Also at École des Beaux Arts, Brussels. Came to United States in 1886. Did Battle Monument at Lake George, New York; Lord Baltimore Monument, Baltimore; statue of Governor Stevens T. Mason in Detroit; and McKinley Monument in Toledo, Ohio.

ROBERT ALEXANDER WEINMANN, NA, sculptor, b 1915. Born in New York, son of sculptor Adolph Alexander Weinmann. Studied at National Academy of Design. Work to be found at Staten Island Community College in New York City and executed Stations of the Cross at Manhattanville College, Purchase, New York.

ARTHUR REGINALD WILLETT, painter, 1868–?. Born in England. Assistant to Edwin Howland Blashfield.

EZRA WINTER, NA, painter, 1886–1949. Born in Manistee, Michigan. Attended the Chicago Academy of Art and was 1911 fellow at the American Academy in Rome. His mural decoration is to be found in Cunard Building and Radio Music Hall, both in New York. Formerly found in old New York Cotton Exchange on Hanover Square and at 40 Wall Street, New York, several of murals formerly at 40 Wall Street now in collection of Smithsonian Institution. Also in Eastman Theater and Monroe County Savings Bank, both in Rochester, New York; Union Trust Building, Detroit; George Rogers Clark Memorial in Vincennes, Indiana; and National Chamber of Commerce in Washington, D.C.

Thomas Jefferson Building   Floor-space area   600,000 square feet
13.7 acres
55,760 square meters

Collections shelving length   547,325 linear feet
104 miles
168 kilometers

John Adams Building   Floor-space area   713,000 square feet
16.4 acres
66,265 square meters

Collections shelving length   954,850 linear feet
180 miles
290 kilometers

James Madison Memorial Building   Floor-space area   1,500,000 square feet
34.5 acres
139,405 square meters

Collections shelving length   1,305,600 linear feet
248 miles
400 kilometers

All Buildings (TJB, JAB, JMMB)   Floor-space area   2,813,000 square feet
64.6 acres
261,430 square meters

Collections shelving length   2,807,775 linear feet
532 miles
858 kilometers

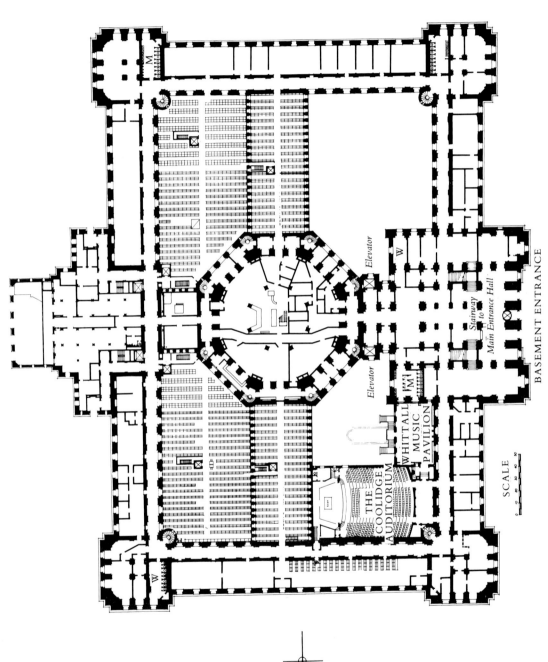

THE LIBRARY OF CONGRESS BASEMENT FLOOR PLAN

BASEMENT ENTRANCE

Elevator

W

Elevator

Stairway to Main Entrance Hall

THE COOLIDGE AUDITORIUM

WHITTALL MUSIC PAVILION

M

W

SCALE
0 10 20 30 40 50

N

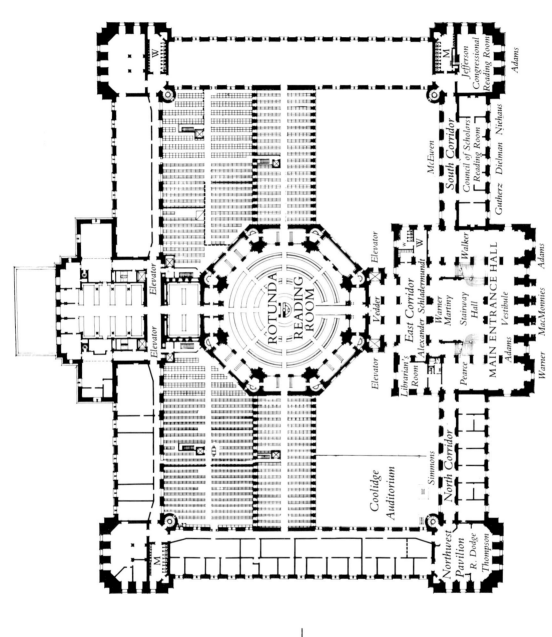

N

LIBRARY OF CONGRESS FIRST FLOOR PLAN

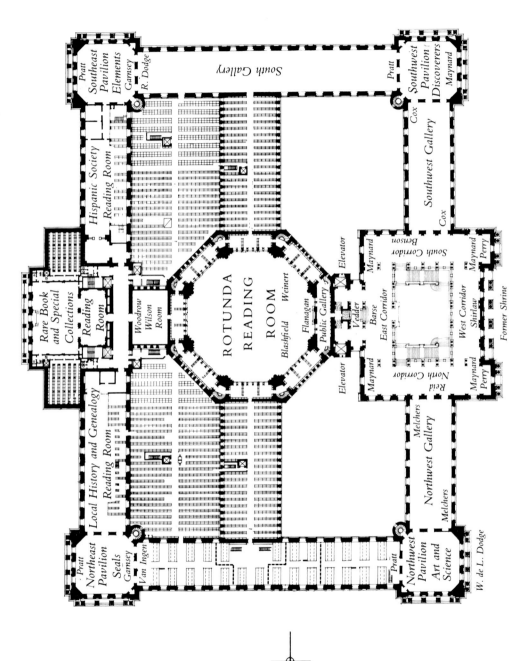

LIBRARY OF CONGRESS SECOND FLOOR PLAN

Pratt
*Southeast Pavilion
Elements*
Garnsey
R. Dodge

South Gallery

Pratt
*Southwest Pavilion
Discoverers*
Maynard

*Hispanic Society
Reading Room*

Cox
Southwest Gallery
Cox

*Rare Book
and Special
Collections
Reading
Room*

*Woodrow
Wilson
Room*

ROTUNDA
READING
ROOM

Blashfield Weinert

Flanagan

Public Gallery

Elevator

Maynard

*South Corridor
Benson*

Vedder

Barse

East Corridor

West Corridor
Shirlaw

Maynard
Perry

Former Shrine

Elevator

Maynard

Reid *North Corridor*

Maynard
Perry

*Local History and Genealogy
Reading Room*

Pratt
*Northeast Pavilion
Seals*
Garnsey
Van Ingen

Pratt
*Northwest Pavilion
Art and
Science*
W. de L. Dodge

Melchers
Northwest Gallery
Melchers

Maynard
Perry

N

215